Genetic Diseases and Developmental Disabilities

Aspects of Detection and Prevention

AAAS Selected Symposia Series

Published by Westview Press
5500 Central Avenue, Boulder, Colorado

for the

American Association for the Advancement of Science
1776 Massachusetts Ave., N.W., Washington, D.C.

Genetic Diseases and Developmental Disabilities

Aspects of Detection and Prevention

Edited by
Tamah L. Sadick and Siegfried M. Pueschel

AAAS Selected Symposium **33**

AAAS Selected Symposia Series

Published in 1979 in the United States of America by
  Westview Press, Inc.
  5500 Central Avenue
  Boulder, Colorado   80301
  Frederick A. Praeger, Publisher

Library of Congress Catalog Card Number: 79-953
ISBN: 0-89158-367-X

Printed and bound in the United States of America

About the Book

Advances in medical genetics during the past two decades have made possible the detection and prevention of many genetic disorders and developmental disabilities. The emphasis of this book is on the application of these new developments to real-life situations. Covering homozygote newborn screening, heterozygote detection in the community, and prenatal diagnostic techniques such as ultrasonography, amniocentesis, and fetal blood sampling, a distinguished group of professionals reviews a subject that has critical implications for individuals, families, and the future of humankind.

About the Series

    The *AAAS Selected Symposia Series* was begun in 1977 to
provide a means for more permanently recording and more
widely disseminating some of the valuable material which is
discussed at the AAAS Annual National Meetings. The volumes
in this *Series* are based on symposia held at the Meetings
which address topics of current and continuing significance,
both within and among the sciences, and in the areas in which
science and technology impact on public policy. The *Series*
format is designed to provide for rapid dissemination of
information, so the papers are not typeset but are reproduced
directly from the camera-copy submitted by the authors, without copy editing. The papers are organized and edited by
the symposium arrangers who then become the editors of the
various volumes. Most papers published in this *Series* are
original contributions which have not been previously published, although in some cases additional papers from other
sources have been added by an editor to provide a more comprehensive view of a particular topic. Symposia may be reports of new research or reviews of established work, particularly work of an interdisciplinary nature, since the AAAS
Annual Meetings typically embrace the full range of the
sciences and their societal implications.

WILLIAM D. CAREY
Executive Officer
American Association for
the Advancement of Science

Contents

List of Figures   xi

List of Tables   xiii

About the Editors and Authors   xv

Introduction-- *Tamah L. Sadick*   1

1   Overview: Genetics and Preventive Medi-
    cine-- *Barton Childs*   7

        References   10

PART I: PREVENTION THROUGH SCREENING AND
        CARRIER DETECTION

2   Genetic Screening: The Heterozygote
    Experience-- *Charles R. Scriver*   13

        Medical and Genetic Paradigms
            of Disease   14
        Genetic Screening   19
        Education of Advocates and
            Clients   26
        References and Notes   29
        Acknowledgements   30

3   Screening of Newborn Infants-- *Robert
    Guthrie*   31

        Introduction   31
        Multiple Tests and Regional-
            ization   33
            Mass Screening for the Hemo-
            globinopathies, 36

Future Possibilities   37
Conclusions   42
References   43

4   Screening for Alpha-1-antitrypsin De-
    ficiency-- *Richard C. Talamo*   45

    Introduction   45
    Genetics   45
    Experience in Alpha-1-
       antitrypsin Screening   46
    Conclusions   47
    References   48

5   Carrier Detection in Duchenne Muscular
    Dystrophy and Implications for Genetic
    Counseling in X-linked Disease--
    Marie-Louise E. Lubs, P. Michael Conneally,
    Kenneth W. Dumars, Robert M. Greenstein, and
    W. Angus Muir   51

    Introduction   51
    CPK Levels and the Diagnosis
       of Duchenne Muscular Dys-
       trophy   52
    Carrier Detection   52
    Clinical Indications of
       Carrier State   56
    Conclusions   61
    References   62

PART II: RECENT ADVANCES AND EXPERIENCE IN
         PRENATAL DIAGNOSIS

6   Prenatal Diagnosis of Chromosomal Dis-
    orders-- *Siegfried M. Pueschel*   65

    References   72

7   Prenatal Detection of Neural Tube Defects
    -- *Aubrey Milunsky (as summarized by Tamah*
    L. Sadick)   75

    References   85

8   Prenatal Diagnosis by Fetoscopy and Fetal
       Blood Sampling Including Initial At-
       tempts to Diagnose Duchenne Muscular
       Dystrophy-- *Maurice J. Mahoney and John C.*
       Hobbins   89

       Fetoscopy   89
         Diagnosis by Fetoscopy,92
       Fetal Blood Sampling   93
         Diagnosis by Fetal Blood Sampling,
         95
       Fetal Skin Biopsy   96
       Risks of Fetoscopy and Fetal
         Blood Sampling   96
       Duchenne Muscular Dystrophy   97
       Summary   98
       References   99

9   Prenatal Diagnosis of the Hemoglobino-
       pathies-- *David G. Nathan, Blanche P. Alter*
       and Maurice J. Mahoney   101

       References   107

PART III: BRIDGING THE GAP BETWEEN RESEARCH
            AND PRACTICE: EDUCATIONAL
            IMPLICATIONS

10 A Place for Genetics in Health Education
       and Vice-Versa-- *Barton Childs*   111

       Modern Views of Medicine and
         Health   113
       Genetics and the New Medicine   115
       Medical Practice   115
       Education in Genetics for
         Physicians and the Public   119
         Medical Teaching,120; The Public,
         120; Genetics in Primary and
         Secondary Schools,121
       What Is To Be Done?   123
         Teaching Population Genetics,
         125; The Public,126
       Conclusion   129
       References   131

List of Figures

Chapter 2

Figure 1   Spectrum of human diseases   16

Figure 2   Types of classification of screening test
            results; statistical classification of
            quantitative phenotypes   20

Figure 3   Method for determining probability of
            assignment for a test result in the
            univariate case with quantitative pheno-
            type distributions   22

Chapter 3

Figure 1   NARC poster children   32

Figure 2   Punch-index machine (1967 model)   34

Chapter 5

Figure 1   Log CPK in serum of carriers for
            Duchenne muscular dystrophy and controls   54

Figure 2   Log CPK in adult and pediatric controls   54

Figure 3   Example of a pedigree   59

Chapter 7

Figure 1   AFP concentrations in neural tube defects   78

Chapter 8

Figure 1   Two fetal toes at 18 weeks (menstrual)
             gestation   90

Figure 2   Diagram of the distal end of a fetoscope
             with a blood sampling needle in a
             placental blood vessel   94

List of Tables

Chapter 2

Table 1   Disease as the enemy and medicine as a war   14

Chapter 3

Table 1   Comparison of cost of screening and treat-
           ment and savings of lifetime care costs   40

Chapter 5

Table 1   Mean CPK in females with a 50% prior risk
           of being carriers for Duchenne muscular
           dystrophy   56

Table 2   Average measurements in carriers of the
           gene for Duchenne muscular dystrophy and
           controls   58

Table 3   CPK levels in obligate carriers in relation
           to physical fitness   58

Table 4   Relative risk of being a carrier for
           Duchenne muscular dystrophy   60

Chapter 9

Table 1   Prenatal diagnosis of hemoglobinopathies,
           July, 1974-February, 1978   104

Table 2   Prenatal diagnosis of hemoglobinopathies,
           July, 1974-June, 1978   105

Chapter 10

Table 1   Medical and pediatric journals offer
           ample space for papers on genetics   116

Table 2   Journals in several medical and allied
           fields publish only occasional articles
           with genetic content, or none at all   118

Table 3   Subjects of articles which appeared in
           Time magazine under the headings Medicine
           and Science, 1969-1972   122

Table 4   Science texts for elementary school students
           do not expose children to much human
           biology   124

About the Editors and Authors

Tamah L. Sadick is a geneticist at the Child Development Center at Rhode Island Hospital and a clinical instructor of pediatrics at Brown University. Her main areas of interest are human and medical genetics and the relationship of genetics to behavior. She is responsible for developing programs and courses in prevention and management of genetic disease, birth defects, and developmental disabilities for undergraduates, professionals, and the health consumer.

Siegfried M. Pueschel, director of the Child Development Center at Rhode Island Hospital, has worked extensively in the areas of developmental disabilities, child development, genetic disorders, Down's syndrome, and amino acid disorders. He is the author of some ten articles on these subjects and has edited a book entitled **Down's Syndrome: Growing and Learning** *(Sheed, Andrews & McMeel, 1978).*

Blanche P. Alter, associate professor of pediatrics at Harvard Medical School, associate in medicine in the Division of Hematology and Oncology at Children's Hospital Medical Center in Boston and a specialist in pediatric hematology, is also senior clinical associate at the Sidney Farber Cancer Institute. She received a U.S. Public Health Service Research Career Development Award to study hemoglobin regulation and differentiation during development (1975-1980) and is the author of some 30 papers on pediatric hematology.

Barton Childs, professor of pediatrics at Johns Hopkins University, is a specialist in pediatrics and genetics.

P. Michael Conneally, professor of medical genetics at the Indiana University School of Medicine, is a specialist in human population genetics. He is the author of numerous publications, especially in the areas of genetic linkage analysis, analysis of family data, and genetic counseling.

Kenneth W. Dumars is associate professor and chief of the Division of Developmental Disabilities and Clinical Genetics at the University of California-Irvine College of Medicine. A member of several professional societies, he has published articles on prenatal diagnosis and genetic counseling, prenatal diagnosis of chromosomal and enzymatic defects, fetal sex determination, the effects of parental drug use on chromosomes of progeny, and other topics.

Robert M. Greenstein is on the staff of the University of Connecticut Health Center in Farmington, Connecticut.

Robert Guthrie, professor of pediatrics and microbiology at the State University of New York at Buffalo and at Children's Hospital, Buffalo, is a specialist in biochemical genetics and mental retardation. A member of several professional societies, he received the American Association on Mental Deficiency Science Award in 1970 and the Kimble Methodology Award in 1965. He is the author of over 50 papers in his areas of expertise.

John C. Hobbins, associate professor of obstetrics and gynecology and of diagnostic radiology at Yale University School of Medicine, is a specialist in perinatology. He is a director of the Society of Perinatal Obstetricians, a fellow of the American College of Obstetrics and Gynecology, and a diplomate of the American Board of Obstetricians and Gynecologists. He has written articles on such topics as fetal blood sampling, ultrasound diagnosis, fetoscopy, and echocardiography, and is coauthor of Ultrasound in Obstetrics and Gynecology *(Williams and Wilkins, 1977).*

Marie-Louise E. Lubs, geneticist and assistant professor of pediatrics in the Department of Pathology at Children's Hospital in Denver, specializes in human genetics. She is a member of the American Society of Human Genetics and the Western Society for Pediatric Research, and has published four books, including Medical Complications of Pregnancy *(Saunders, 1975) and* Genetic Counseling *(Raven, 1976).*

Maurice J. Mahoney, associate professor of human genetics and pediatrics at Yale University School of Medicine, specializes in prenatal diagnosis, inborn errors of metabolism, and somatic cell genetics. He has published articles on metabolism of organic acids, vitamin B_{12} and porphyrins; diagnosis and treatment of genetic diseases during fetal life; development of fetoscopy; and fetal blood sampling for clinical application.

Aubrey Milunsky is director of the Genetics Division at the Eunice Kennedy Shriver Center and Harvard Medical School.

He is the author of over 100 articles and 7 books, including The Prevention of Genetic Disease and Mental Retardation *(Saunders, 1975),* Genetic Disorders and the Fetus: Diagnosis, Prevention and Treatment *(Plenum, in press), and* Advances in Perinatal Medicine, Vol. 1 *(Plenum, in preparation).*

W. Angus Muir, assistant professor of medicine and director of the Division of Human Genetics at Case Western Reserve University, is also a genetic counselor at the Muscular Dystrophy Clinic. He is a member of several professional organizations including the American Society of Human Genetics.

David G. Nathan, chief of the Division of Hematology and Oncology at Children's Hospital Medical Center and the Sidney Farber Cancer Institute in Boston, is also professor of pediatrics at Harvard Medical School and pediatrician-in-chief at the Sidney Farber Cancer Institute. He is a director of the Medical Foundation, Inc., councillor of the American Society of Hematology, and chairman of the Advisory Committee on Childhood Cancer, American Cancer Society-Massachusetts Division, and of the Massachusetts Commission on Human Clinical Investigation and Experimental Therapy. He serves on the editorial boards of numerous professional journals and has published some 160 articles.

Charles R. Scriver, professor of biology of the Faculty of Science and professor of pediatrics on the Faculty of Medicine at McGill University, specializes in human biochemical genetics. A member of many professional organizations, he received the Mead-Johnson Award in 1969 and the Borden Award in 1974. He is the author of over 200 articles and reviews on membrane transport, human biochemical genetics, inborn errors of metabolism, genetic screening, and related fields, and a monograph, Amino Acid Metabolism and Its Disorders *(with L.E. Rosenberg; Saunders, 1973).*

Richard C. Talamo, Eudowood Professor of Pediatric Pulmonary Diseases at the Johns Hopkins University School of Medicine, specializes in allergy and immunology as well as pediatric pulmonary diseases. He is chairman of the Pediatric Assembly of the American Thoracic Society, chairman of the Cystic Fibrosis Foundation Research Committee, and a fellow of the American Academy of Allergy and of the American Academy of Pediatrics. He has published articles on emphysema and alpha-1-antitrypsin deficiency, cystic fibrosis, and the kallikrein-kinin system and two books: Cystic Fibrosis and Related Diseases *(Intercontinental, 1973) and* Cystic Fibrosis: Projections into the Future *(Intercontinental, 1977).*

Introduction

Tamah L. Sadick

The primary aim of this volume is to inform a general scientific audience, including professionals in education, medicine, and in other allied health fields of several of the dramatic advances which have been made in the field of human and medical genetics within the past 10 to 15 years and the role that these advances play in the detection and prevention of disease, in the maintenance of health, and in the improvement of the quality of life. Internationally renowned physicians and geneticists describe, analyze, and discuss the progress made in their respective fields.

We are witnessing the gradual change from a primarily disease-oriented medical profession into a more health-oriented one. As nutritional and infectious diseases become better understood and managed, genetic disorders assume a greater relative importance. The innovative technologies in cytogenetics and biochemical genetics permit investigations in human genetics previously undreamed of. Of equal importance is the increased awareness of health maintenance among large segments of educated consumers. These and other factors have a common focus: to improve the quality of life of the individual human being.

While an ever increasing aggregate of knowledge in medical genetics is filling journals and programs of scientific meetings, this information is often neither imparted to the practitioner nor communicated in a comprehensible way to society. A large gap between the known basic technology and its maximum use by the professional and consumer is still very great. This volume is an effort towards narrowing that gap.

The first section of this volume is devoted to the implications of homozygote and heterozygote screening and the second section to the most recent advances and issues in prenatal diagnosis. The moral, ethical, legal, religious, and psychosocial issues, all of which have known constraints on the utilization of these techniques, are covered only briefly. More fully covered are the educational implications of the scientific advances and the impact that the genetic approach to human disease can have at all levels of health care.

In the first paper, Dr. Childs so poignantly sets the tone for this monograph focusing on our principle message "the preventive elements in genetics" and the role that they can play in a "reorientation of preventive medicine". His emphasis is on the underlying principle that most diseases will be found to be "a misfit of genotypes and environment" not an hypothesis that is easily documented at this time. This is in contrast to disorders expressed as a result of the action of single mutant genes or chromosomal abnormalities where the greatest advances in detection and prevention to date have been made.

Dr. Scriver follows with an eloquent presentation on the medical and genetic paradigm of disease, attacking, as Dr. Childs does, the traditional medical approach, particularly when discussing the vast amount of genetic variation and heterogeneity found in mankind. He emphasizes that "we are not all created equal--biologically". His discussion of heterozygosity includes the hypothesis that some genes, if allowed to interact with some adverse environmental conditions, may cause serious chronic debilitating disease.

Both Dr. Childs and Dr. Scriver emphasize the importance of Darwin's and Mendel's messages. They point out that although information cannot solve everything, it is the least common denominator if people at all educational levels are to work with the professional towards maintenance of their own health and the health and well being of their offspring.

Highlighting the approach to homozygote screening, Dr. Robert Guthrie goes beyond the phenylketonuria screening of newborn children and discusses the broader applications of homozygote screening. He realized that in order for newborn screening to be widely available it had to be sensitive, specific, simple, accurate, replicable, and cost-effective. He developed the dried filter paper bacterial inhibition assay, which fits all these criteria and which could be extended to several other now treatable metabolic diseases. He then points to the future of a well-organized national endeavor in the United States in the approach to newborn screening.

Thus, the same criteria--reliability, sensitivity, simplicity, accuracy, replicability, and cost-effectiveness--as used for homozygote screening on a wide basis should be applied to both heterozygote screening of all types and also to the techniques used in prenatal diagnosis. Unfortunately, biochemical and cytogenetic technology has not advanced as rapidly in some of these areas nor have the correlations between genotype and disease susceptibility and/or health become clearly understood.

Thus, in his discussion on screening for alpha-1 antitrypsin deficiency, Dr. Richard Talamo provides an overview of today's knowledge concerning this complex genetic disorder and its relationship to environmental factors. He describes the genotype and elaborates on the clinical aspects of alpha-1 antitrypsin deficiency and heterogeneity. Dr. Talamo also reminds us that much research still needs to be done to arrive at a better understanding of this disease entity. Because of the lack of treatment, he advises against the initiation of large scale screening programs at the present time.

In the next paper, Dr. Lubs and her colleagues analyze the present state of the art with respect to carrier detection in Duchenne muscular dystrophy and the implications for genetic counseling for X-linked disease. Here again there are obstacles in carrier detection which result in great difficulties in counseling some of the tested individuals. According to Lubs and coworkers, most carrier tests for X-linked recessive disorders are of limited value because of the overlap between carriers and controls caused by Lyonization.

The second section of the volume is devoted to recent advances in the prevention of serious, presently untreatable genetic disease, through the use of prenatal diagnosis. The techniques include, in addition to amniocentesis and ultrasound, placental aspiration, fetoscopy, and fetal blood sampling. At the present time, prevention of the birth of defective individuals is the only recourse in preventing many genetic diseases though treatment in utero or in the early neonatal period would be a more desirable alternative.

In the first two chapters of this section, Drs. Pueschel and Milunsky discuss amniocentesis in terms of chromosomal disorders and neural tube defects (NTD's). This technique has proved to be the safest, most reliable, accurate, and relatively cost-effective of all the antenatal diagnostic methods. It is the most widely used prenatal diagnostic technique and has been highly instrumental in revolutionizing the practice of clinical genetics and genetic counseling.

Although in theory all numerical and structural chromosomal aberrations, 90% of neural tube defects and between
60-80 inborn errors of metabolism have the potential for
detection prenatally, amniocentesis still remains underutilized almost everywhere for various reasons. However, it
is emphasized in this volume that amniocentesis, usually
accompanied by ultrasound as an adjunctive technique, has
proven most effective in allowing couples known to be at
high reproductive risk for certain diseases, to selectively
choose, without fear, to have children of their own free at
least of that genetic disorder in question.

Milunsky further discusses mass screening for maternal
serum alpha-fetoprotein to detect neural tube defects
(NTD's). Through this type of screening, the potential of
reaching individuals before they have an affected child is
made possible. Screening of maternal serum is now part of
routine obstetrical care in the United Kingdom, and the implications of this for a nationwide program in the United
States are discussed. As valuable a tool as maternal serum
screening for NTD's is proving to be in the United Kingdom
and in a smaller study conducted in the United States, it
may have the potential for even greater value in detecting
early in gestation high-risk pregnancies which may result
in prematurity, multiple births, and/or low birth weight
babies.

Though heterozygote detection for carriers of the recessive genes and homozygote detection of those affected
with one or the other of the hemoglobinopathies have been
available for a number of years to specific ethnic populations, no prenatal diagnosis was available. Thus, the only
alternatives open to couples, both of whom were found to be
carriers of one of the hemoglobinopathies, was to have no
children, to take their chances for having a normal or an
affected child, or to resort to artificial insemination.
The success for prevention of Tay-Sachs disease through
carrier detection and prenatal diagnosis was not reproducible
for sickle cell disease or B-thalassemia because fetal blood
tissue, necessary for their detection, was unobtainable
through amniocentesis.

Drs. Mahoney, Nathan, and their colleagues discuss the
newer techniques of fetoscopy, placental aspiration, and
fetal blood sampling and the accompanying sophisticated laboratory procedures which opened up the possibility for detection in utero of these diseases. An initial effort has
been made to diagnose Duchenne muscular dystrophy in utero

as well. However, these techniques are more invasive, risky,
and more costly than amniocentesis, not the prerequisites we
have mentioned for techniques that can gain widespread usage
in detection and prevention although they are effective and
available on an experimental basis.

Drs. Nathan, Alter, and Mahoney look forward hopefully
to the possibility that simple, less invasive tests and
techniques, will be devised in terms of prenatal diagnosis
of sickle cell disease and B-thalassemia; and Drs. Mahoney
and Hobbins further stress the difficulties that have been
encountered in the prenatal detection of Duchenne muscular
dystrophy.

In the final chapter, Dr. Childs again emphasizes the
benefits that may accrue from the available genetic knowledge
if it is applied in human affairs in terms of prevention of
disease and the preservation of biological and social equilibrium. By using the genetic paradigm, Dr. Childs indicates that we may be able to improve genotypes and promote
physical and emotional health. In minimizing the adverse
effects of some genes and maximizing the virtues of others,
the desired quality of life could conceivably be attained.
In order to achieve such goals, Dr. Childs reemphasizes his
belief that the educational approach must be pursued in
order to make health providers and consumers cognizant of
the role genetics may play in avoidance of disease and in
the maintenance of health.

We extend to the scientists who made this volume possible our deepest appreciation and sincere thanks and look
forward to a world made somewhat more comfortable by their
contributions.

Overview
Genetics and Preventive Medicine

Barton Childs

The growth of information about human genetics has pro-
ceeded according to a curve similar to that exhibited by
bacteria or other populations of living organisms. The la-
tency period dates from sometime in the 17th century and the
exponential upturn from the early 1950s. Since then, knowledge has accumulated at an accelerating rate; McKusick's
catalogue lists mutants for upwards of 2000 loci (1); there
are several hundred inborn errors of metabolism, and almost
as many chromosome abnormalities (2); all chromosomes are
identifiable, and the position of more than 200 loci is known
(3); most teaching hospitals have genetics clinics; many, if
not most, medical schools have included genetics in the required curriculum, and 15 or more have given the enterprise
the substance and visibility of department standing. Nor is
there evidence of slackening of the pace of discovery and
expansion of genetic services. In the face of such progress,
it may seem ungracious to wish for more, but the fact is that
these developments are altogether in the conventional medical
mode; that is, genetics is perceived as a medical subspecial-
ty and the genes are given an etiological role analogous to
that of bacteria or of toxic substances. But this is a parochial and typological view of the significance of genetics,
whether for medicine or mankind. It is parochial because it
focuses so strongly on gene action at the expense of other
aspects of variation, and typological because it makes too
unambiguous a distinction between health and disease and
forces genetics into an anachronistic and exclusionary classification of diseases according to their "genetic" or "environmental" origins. Medical geneticists are not without
responsibility for this limited viewpoint. The genetics
clinic, for all its convenience and efficiency, is mute confirmation of the specialty label, and if we use the designa-
tion of genetic disease as shorthand for 'a disease in which
mutant genes have made a particular person unfit to maintain
homeostasis in the face of specified conditions,' a non-

geneticist may be pardoned for failing to decipher the shorthand. What is needed is a slight change in emphasis, a recognition that although there are a few disorders in which the
action of mutant genes disrupts homeostasis independently of
any imaginable conditions, and some circumstances against
which no imaginable genotype is proof, the vast bulk of disease is the result of a misfit of genotypes and environments. Neither genotype nor environment is of itself good or
bad, such value judgements actually have meaning only for affected individuals and their relatives, but such evaluations
become general when the number of affected persons reaches
some level of medical or public notice, and certain genes are
then called deleterious and some environmental conditions or
substances are called bad, and the warning goes out that
something should be taken off the market or some "lifestyle"
should be changed. But if some mutants are deleterious only
in the face of some conditions, and some experiences are bad
for only some genotypes, perhaps the most important message
genetics has for medicine is "discover the possessors of the
mutants and find appropriate conditions of living for their
bearers." That is, it is my belief that in another generation it will be apparent that the most significant contribution of genetics to human welfare was a new orientation of
preventive medicine. As things stand, moderation, even ab-
stinence, is pressed upon us all. Such counsel, which ig-
nores human variability, is almost certain to be only par-
tially effective, but if directed to those whose self-
interest is most clearly involved, that is, those shown to be
genetically susceptible or predisposed, it may have more
chance. I should add that this is still largely an hypothesis, not having been widely tested yet, but it is more plaus-
ible than that <u>everyone</u> should heed warnings about hazards
which each person's intuition suggests are remote, or will,
in any case, affect someone else. It is also not a new
hypothesis, dating at least to the 15th century when it was
so pointedly presented in the nursery rhyme about the Sprats.
Jack Sprat, you will recall, could eat no fat, and his wife
could eat no lean, and so between the two of them they licked
the platter clean. Well, perhaps Jack had familial hypercholesterolemia, while his wife was a heterozygote for one of
the sex-linked protein intolerances, and so they made a virtue of necessity observing the best principles of preventive
medicine.

     I said all that is required to adopt this point of view
is a slight change in emphasis, but matters of emphasis far
more subtle than this have furnished history with some of its
most brutal and sanguinary struggles. How the shift is to be
implemented is not clear, although in time its rational appeal is likely to be convincing, even if no systematic

efforts were made, but some more rapid progress might occur
if those most directly involved in preventive medicine were
to perceive it; that is, those engaged in the practice of
primary medical care.

The evolution of preventive medicine and its present
conjunction with primary care is strikingly similar to that
of human genetics. Originating in the 19th century in efforts by government or voluntary agencies to preserve the
health of the public through social action, including im-
provements in sanitation, housing, nutrition, and working
conditions, preventive medicine, like genetics, entered its
exonential phase in the 1950s (4). Since then, the separation between prevention of disease by government or other
agencies and treatment by medical practitioners has become
blurred as the latter have begun to perceive the maintenance
of health as one of their duties, and as the need for some
sort of unitary system for the provision of health services
has become apparent. Many steps in this direction have been
taken, especially during the past 10-15 years; including
medicare, medicaid, group practices, and health maintenance
organizations where screening practices can be carried on,
and in schools of medicine, departments of community medicine
and family practice. There is even evidence of a resurgence
of general practice.

The extraordinary thing is that these developments and
those in genetics have been going on in parallel with scarce-
ly a flicker of recognition across invisible, intangible
boundaries. Geneticists have discovered how to use their
discipline in the pursuit of preventive goals, but academic
officialdom in prevention has perceived neither the identity
of their own aims with those of the geneticists, nor the
virtues of the genetic method in realizing those aims. But
others interested in prevention have become engaged with
geneticists in preventive measures. Officials of state health
departments have been quick to see the value of screening for
disease and for heterozygotes and to support programs in
treatment, counseling, and antenatal diagnosis. This progress has been made possible mainly as a result of transactions between state and city health departments and voluntary agencies, on the one hand, and physician-geneticists
lodged usually in departments of pediatrics or obstetrics, on
the other. But the evidence is that the relevant academic
departments in medical schools, and primary care physicians
in practice, have been slow to see how they might be involved in these new forms of medical care or that the future
is sure to bring a vast expansion of such services (5). I
think two related forces will change this. One is the threat
of malpractice suits which, like the prospect of hanging,

concentrates the mind wonderfully; and the second is public demand. The public is in the process of being apprised, sometimes inaccurately, of the value of genetic services, and the clamor will increase. So, to my mind, the way that shift in emphasis will occur is through the spread of preventive services in which people with special hereditary qualities will be found and advised, whether to adopt some new mode of living or to avoid some particular experience or that, given their genotype and that of their mates, certain reproductive outcomes may be expected with certain probabilities. And little by little a fundamental question in medicine will take on a new form. Instead of asking "What is the cause of such and such a disease, and how do we treat it?", we will ask "What are the reasons why this person has such and such a disease, or is predisposed to it, and how can we treat him or help him to manage his life so as to avoid it?"

References

1. McKusick, V.A.: Mendelian Inheritance in Man, 4th Ed., Johns Hopkins Press, Baltimore, 1975.

2. Borgaonkar, D.S.: Chromosomal Variation in Man, Johns Hopkins Press, Baltimore, 1975

3. McKusick, V.A. and Ruddle, F.H.: The status of the gene map of the human chromosomes. Science 196:390-405, 1977

4. Rosen, G.: Preventive Medicine in the United States, 1900-1975, Science History Publications, New York, 1975

5. Childs, B.: Persistent echoes of the nature-nurture argument. American Journal of Human Genetics 29:1-13, 1977

Part I

Prevention Through Screening and Carrier Detection

Genetic Screening

The Heterozygote Experience

Charles R. Scriver

Two quotations from Juvenal (1), the Roman satirist,
introduce my contribution to this symposium.

What good are family trees?   (Satire VIII)

What a grossly ravening maw
That man must have who dines off whole roast boar - a beast
Ordained for convivial feasting! But you'll pay the price
All too too soon, my friend, when you undress and waddle
Into the bath, your belly still swollen with undigested
Peacock-meat - a lightning heart attack, with no time
To make your final will.
                    (Satire I)

Juvenal wrote the Satires as a series of moral
portraits for an age which - in some ways - was not unlike
our own. By "family tree" in the first quotation, we
presume he meant social lineage. But in our age the term
refers also to biological lineage, and we do care about the
family tree, because it may contain information we need to
prevent inherited disease. In the second quotation the
satirist paints a grotesque vignette to limn a general
lesson on lifestyle. Yet even moral men have lightning,
premature heart attacks - when they have special risks to
their personal health. Their family tree - not their
morality - can set those risks upon them.

Most of us are not likely to believe we have
genetically - determined risks to our own health. Such
risks tend to make ourselves "the enemy"; and we are not
conditioned to enjoy that message.

Medical and Genetic Paradigms of Disease

We have been taught to wage war upon disease; and why not? Past crusades and campaigns against scourges have been very successful. Causes of disease (the enemy) have been identified; cures mobilized. Polio has been eradicated; smallpox vanquished; entrenched infections routed. We use the language of World War I to describe our victorious attacks on disease (Table 1). Past campaigns have changed the pattern of contemporary disease in developed countries. Degenerative diseases, malignancies, hereditary problems and birth defects now dominate the disease profiles of these nations, and now, we wage new wars on these stubborn ailments. But where is the cause of cancer? What agent causes the premature heart attack? How do we cure birth defects? How do we understand the enemy when it is partly ourselves. Our cherished medical paradigms fail us when we try to understand.

The traditional medical approach to disease fails us because we tend to ignore the fact that we are not all created equal - biologically. We need a new declaration of independence creating a state of awareness of our biological rights. The declaration might begin by recognizing that

Table 1

DISEASE as the ENEMY

and

MEDICINE as a WAR

The language we use:

... killer disease

... breakthrough discovery/treatment

... crush . . .

... eradicate . . .

... (cobalt) bomb

... war on (cancer/polio/ . . .)

... entrenched infection . . .

---

women are different from men. It would recognize that human
beings are freighted with genetic variation; some of it
advantageous under particular circumstances - as for example
in the case of sickle cell trait in a falciparum malaria
environment; most of it neutral under the general conditions
of life; a bit of it responsible for actual or potential
harm - such as the mutation causing abnormal membrane
receptor activity for the LDL-cholesterol complex.

Rapid growth of knowledge about the inborn errors of
metabolism in the past quarter century, and an initial
modest success with screening and treatment of affected
homozygotes for a few Mendelian diseases, has dramatized
these rare examples of human biochemical variation.
Although about 2500 other Mendelian traits and disorders
have now been catalogued (2), we tend to view them all for
what they are - an aggregate of outlier events at a remote
end of the disease spectrum (Figure 1). In this spectrum,
expression of rare mutant genes in the universal environment
occupies one end while the effect of a particular
environment upon individuals of universal genotype occupies
the other. In the middle lie the common multifactorial
diseases which fill our hospital beds. *The underlying theme
is that particular genes confer special risks for many of
these common diseases. To put it another way, it is
heterozygotes who tend to fill our hospital beds.*

We have begun to act rather confidently on behalf of
the homozygotes among us. We design programs for the
screening, diagnosis, counseling and treatment of them - for
example in the prevention of phenylketonuria. We even
recognize that genetic heterogeneity is the rule rather than
the exception among the inborn errors of metabolism (3).
We know that the recognition of heterogeneity is important,
because it guides us to titrate the environment precisely
to the tolerance of the mutant individual in the process of
treatment. Accordingly, we are relatively comfortable in
this microcosm of extreme genetic variation because its
significance is understood (4).

And yet we are uneasy with the broader, but equivalent,
concept of prevalent heterozygosity - or polymorphism - in
the apparently healthy population. For example, Harris and
colleagues found extensive polymorphism at the gene loci
responsible for normal acid phosphatase activity in red
blood cells (5). With an electrophoretic method they
demonstrated six different patterns of acid phosphatase to
account for the frequency distribution of enzyme activity
among individuals in a British Caucasian population. These
investigators went on to show comparable genetic variation

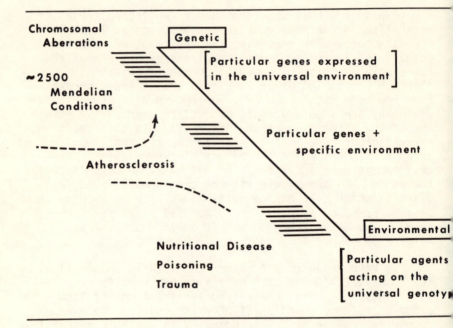

Figure 1. Spectrum of human diseases to emphasise those of primarily intrinsic origin (top left) or extrinsic origin (bottom right) and those of multifactorial origin (middle).

at one third of the gene loci they examined (6,7). They calculated an average heterozygosity per gene locus of at least 6.7%. After taking into account the limitation of electrophoretic methods to detect Mendelian variation in proteins, they predicted the average heterozygosity per human gene locus is close to 20 percent.

We are not yet in a position to interpret the biological significance of most of this heterozygosity. But we can't ignore it. We are due to learn about it, as we have learned about the meaning of genetic heterogeneity in our party pieces - the inborn errors of metabolism.

Heterozygotes for autosomal recessive diseases such as phenylketonuria, Tay-Sachs disease and sickle cell anemia constitute between two and ten percent of the community in which the disease is found; the medical significance of that fact has only recently been perceived. Now we must extend the concept of heterozygosity to include virtually everyone in the population and to realize that heterozygosity in relation to a particular environment may influence the health of the individual.

The traditional view of how disease occurs is in transition. The medical paradigm of cause does not explain many common ailments and it offers no option for cure. The genetic paradigm of special inherited risks for particular individuals is often a more useful interpretation and it can sometimes provide the option for prevention.

The genetic paradigm views health as an equilibrium between the genome-or our "nature", and the environment-or our "nurture". Disease is disequilibrium, sometimes caused by an excess of the environment, at other times the result of a change in the fulcrum controlling equilibrium. In the paradigm, the gene product is the fulcrum; it determines the equilibrium between the biological function and the environmental force acting upon the organism.

Consider three Mendelian examples of the genetic paradigm.

1. Porphyria variegata is associated with life-threatening neurologic crisis. Exposure to barbiturates precipitates the crises. The aberrant function is a step in the biosynthesis of porphyrin.

2. Hemolytic anemia is provoked by exposure to the antimalarial primaquin or other oxidant agents. The aberrant function is an enzyme in the pentose

pathway of red blood cells.

3. Emphysema is probably more prevalent in smokers with α_1 antitrypsin deficiency; aberrant protease inhibitor activity in the presence of a chronic irritant environment permits lung damage.

In each case the health of a heterozygous person is at risk because of the specific inherited genotype; an environmental event, harmless to most persons, provokes disease in the person at risk. It follows that knowledge of genotype allows one to prescribe a specific course of action or lifestyle that can prevent disease.

So far so good, as long as these examples are confined to the teaching of genetics and don't get in the way of the real business at hand - the practice of medicine. But that attitude just won't do for a world view of human health. The barbiturate risk is pertinent to one-in 400 Afrikaaners and a South African physician is liable to a malpractice suit if his patients receive barbiturates without being screened for porphyria variegata. The primaquin example is relevant to thousands of men living in malarial regions of the world. The smoking risk is still being evaluated and because it could be pertinent to hundreds of thousands, it has earned a place of its own, in this volume.

The larger issues revealed in these examples of genetic variation are important for two reasons. First they suggest that heterozygote screening may become a major medical activity in defining special medical risks for particular individuals. Second they imply that prevalent heterozygosity could be the basis of much disease.

Most citizens are unfamiliar with their own genetic diversity. Therefore we can anticipate a denial of programs designed to reveal it - as we have seen for example in the case of sickle cell screening (8). And most physicians are equally unfamiliar with these concepts; therefore they do not want to know about their patients' genotypes.

How we classify a person as a carrier of a variant gene is a delicate process. It threatens self-image; and it challenges traditional medical practices. Accordingly, the basic principles of screening and classification merit our attention. It is also prudent to know why citizens know so little about their own heterozygosity. If genetics were an item on our personal and national agendas and if screening practices were ideal, I believe we could alleviate the disease burden of modern society rather considerably.

Accordingly, the remainder of this paper is addressed to
problems of classification in screening and public
education in genetics.

Genetic Screening

Genetic screening is a process whose aim is to identify
genetic variation among individuals in populations (9).
Genetic screening is a particular activity within the broad
domain of medical screening. Screening should be
distinguished from the traditional medical act of
surveillance (10). Screening is usually a short-term cross-
sectional activity while surveillance tends to be a long-
term vigil on the health of a person or population. The
person screened should be aware that the acts of screening
and surveillance, in themselves, never confer immunity to
the condition being scrutinized.

Heterozygote screening - in its general form - is a
search in a population for persons at risk for genetic
disease in themselves or their descendants, in either the
universal or a particular environment. On the other hand,
the search may have no other purpose than to gather
information on the frequency distribution of a genetic
variant. The specific objectives for heterozygote screening
are:

First   The detection of those at risk for their own
           health because they possess a particular genetic
           variant and for which screening may provide an
           opportunity for medical intervention to offset the
           effects of gene expression.

Second   The detection of those at risk for passing a
           potentially harmful gene to their offspring and
           for which counseling about reproductive options
           may avert the harm.

Third   The enumeration of gene frequencies in a
           population, often coupled with an investigation of
           the biological significance and genetic
           epidemiology of the variants.

Heterozygote screening for the goal of medical
intervention is illustrated by identification of the
dominantly inherited porphyria phenotype, which allows the
carrier to avoid exposure to barbiturates. Screening for
carriers with deficient LDL-cholesterol binding, while still
experimental, will allow persons at risk for this form of
hypercholesterolemic coronary artery disease to receive

Binary

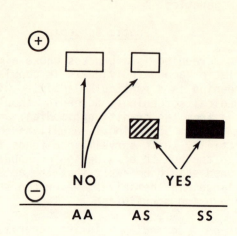

Statistical

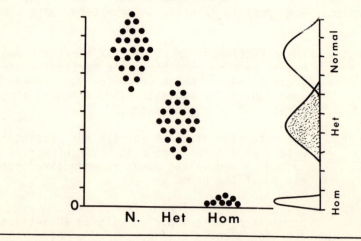

Figure 2. Types of classification of screening test results. Binary classification of qualitative phenotypes for sickle and normal hemoglobin identified by electrophoresis; statistical classification of quantitative phenotypes, e.g. serum hexosaminidase A activity.

pharmacologic regulation of their cholesterol metabolism.

Heterozygote screening for the goal of reproductive counseling is illustrated by Tay-Sachs carrier screening. When prospective parents are both carriers for the Tay-Sachs allele, amniocentesis permits fetal diagnosis in the mid-trimester. If the fetus has the gangliosidosis, termination of the pregnancy is an acceptable option for consideration. In the case of sickle cell anemia or β-thalassemia major, carrier screening serves a similar goal, provided facilities are available to obtain a fetal blood sample, and to examine fetal globin chain synthesis. On the other hand, without the option for precise fetal diagnosis of the hemo-globinopathies, heterozygote screening has had unfortunate repercussions. In this situation such parents, learning that they are at risk for having affected offspring are uncertain as to the outcome of any pregnancy; they may interpret the screening experience to mean they can have no children.

Experimental screening is illustrated by recently completed studies on the prevalence of the deficiency LDL-cholesterol binding allele; and by the ongoing studies of α_1-antitrypsin deficiency.

Screening tests are most efficient when they identify genotypes unequivocally. Accurate discrimination between mutant and wild genotypes is possible when the mutant gene expresses itself in a structural variant of the normal gene product that is recognizable by the screening process. In this case, the screening test recognizes a qualitative phenotype and permits the decision: *change* or *no change* - as for example in the case of screening for hemoglobin S; the process of genotype discrimination is binary (Figure 2).

In most cases the screening test discerns a quantitative phenotype such as enzyme activity or metabolite concentration (Figure 2). The distribution of the quantitative phenotype depends on genotype; mutant and wild phenotypes overlap in cases of unimodal distribution with polygenic inheritance and they may overlap in cases of bimodal distribution with monogenic inheritance. Accordingly, the specific genotype can be identified only with a certain probability which must be calculated. Accurate discrimination of quantitative phenotypes is an important and typical problem in screening programs designed to identify and counsel heterozygotes.

The efficiency of a genetic screening method is related to its specificity and its sensitivity. *Specificity* is defined as the ability to exclude from classification as

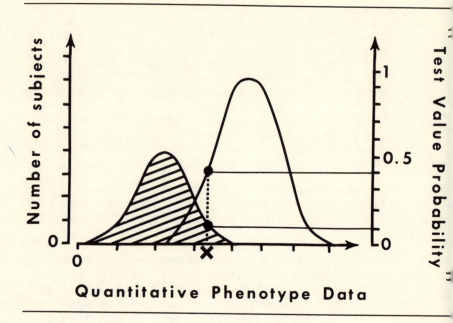

Figure 3. Method for determining probability of assignment for a test result in the univariate case with quantitative phenotype distributions in normal and heterozygous (hatched) populations (see text).

heterozygotes, those who have the normal homozygous genotype. In the screening process, the non carrier may yield either a normal test result (with frequency a) or a positive result (with frequency b), the latter being a *false positive test* result. The specificity of screening is then $\frac{a}{a+b}$.

Sensitivity is defined as the ability of the test to identify those who possess the mutation. The latter yield either a positive test (with frequency d) or a normal (*false negative*) test result (with frequency c). The sensitivity of screening is then $\frac{d}{c+d}$. Binary test systems can yield perfect specificity and sensitivity but quantitative testing may not.

Correct classification of screened individuals by means of their test result is obviously important. The direction of all subsequent medical and genetic counseling is dependent on the genotype assigned. If we are counseling couples for an autosomal recessive phenotype, the concern for correct classification is heightened, since the probability of correct assignment of couples at risk is the square of the probability for correct assignment of individuals.

The example of screening for carrier status in a Tay-Sachs disease prevention program can be used to illustrate different approaches to classification of individuals. Let us assume that the screening program is well run; the serum hexosaminidase assay is properly standardized. Quantitative phenotypic data for a wild-type population have been obtained and the corresponding distribution in a population of obligate heterozygotes is known. The univariate distributions of the heterozygous and wild-type quantitative phenotypes have been plotted and overlap is observed (Figure 3). An individual with value X for hexosaminidase-A activity in serum is to be counseled about his likelihood of heterozygosity (11). The relative frequencies of normal and heterozygous persons with value X is indicated by the relative heights of the distribution curves at X; therefore the "test probability" for being a normal subject is 0.40; and it is 0.10 for heterozygosity in this example (Figure 3). Now, if the screening program which supplied the quantitative phenotype distribution data was developed in a community where the prior frequency of heterozygosity is 4 percent, then the prior probability of being heterozygous is 0.04 - and of having the wild genotype, 0.96. The arithmetic products of prior probability *times* test probability are calculated to determine the probabilities of normal (P_1) and mutant genotypes (P_2) which in this case are 0.384 and 0.004

respectively. The posterior probability of being a carrier
with the test result shown is then $P_2/(P_1+P_2)= 0.0103$ or
about 1%.

In the case of Tay-Sachs heterozygote screening there is
more information available from the analysis of the
quantitative phenotype than the serum hexosaminidase-A
activity alone. In order to estimate the heat-labile
component of hexosaminidase, it is necessary to calculate
total activity first, then to heat the sample under defined
conditions and reassay. Heat-stable and heat-labile
activities in the sample are thus defined. A similar
situation exists in screening for β-thalassemia
heterozygotes (12). Data for five red cell parameters are
routinely obtained by the Coulter Counter and data on the
concentration of Hb A_2 are also available without much
additional effort. These six variables are interrelated and
we have found the combination of mean corpuscular volume and
Hb A_2 to be a particular powerful pair of discriminants (12).
Such non-independent components of information can be used
for classification using that branch of statistics known as
discriminant analysis (13).

Two approaches can be adopted. A mathematic function of
discriminatory measurements could be constructed in terms of
several univariate distributions. The discriminant function
is the linear combination of the variables which yields a
critical value permitting maximum differentiation between the
quantitative phenotypes of heterozygotes and normal subjects.
However a manageable discriminant function may be
inaccessible for various reasons in which case another
approach is required.

An alternate approach serves the explicit purpose of
population screening for autosomal recessive heterozygotes
rather than genetic counseling of the individual. In this
case interpretation of the screening test result can take
into account not only two non-independent biochemical test
results but also the prior probability of the heterozygous
genotype and an arbitrary level of certitude for precise
calculation of counseling error costs in the screening
program. In our approach to β-thalassemia carrier screening
we combined mean red cell volume and Hemoglobin A_2 as well
as the prior probability of carrier status to construct
density functions from which contours of certitude for
classification error of Greek heterozygotes could be
calculated (12). The method is based on the application of
Bayes theorem to probability density functions, and it is
a powerful method serving our Montreal population for
β-thalassemia screening.

In the simple combinatorial method and in the probability density function method, prior probability of heterozygosity is used. In both approaches the test value leads to a statement of posterior probability about genotype assignment. However, the client is unlikely to be very interested in his personal probability statement. His primary concern is; Am I a carrier? It is possible to refine the accuracy of genotype assignment by additional steps, so that the counselor can speak with a maximum certitude that is clear, at least to himself or herself.

In a critical clinical situation where accurate assignment is paramount, quantitative data for offspring or parents of the screenee can assist the counselor. We can readily see how this would be particularly important in the delineation of heterozygotes with defective LDL-cholesterol binding at the present state of the art for screening of this phenotype.

Misclassification of screenees has undesirable consequences both upon the goals of the program and upon self-image of clients. These consequences are the costs of misclassification. In general, it can be said that the error costs of *not* screening and counseling always exceed those that accumulate because of screening (14). Furthermore the cost of counseling on the basis of two tests (the bivariate case) is considerably less than the cost of either corresponding univariate case.

In our own approach to Tay-Sachs carrier screening, for example we adopted the position that the cost of miscounseling a heterozygote was 100 times greater than the cost of miscounseling a normal homozygote (14). We used this assumption to develop the contour defining a certitude of classification in the Tay-Sachs carrier screening program. We calculated the costs of misclassification of heterozygotes against the cost of not counseling knowing that our classification error is 5.9% for the wild genotype and 1.5% for heterozygotes. At 4% heterozygote frequency, the cost of counseling is 0.1159 while the cost of not counseling is 34 fold greater.

Specificity, sensitivity and classification costs in genetic screening have been examined so far in this discussion. What we have been discussing is only a minimum standard for the interpretation of quantitative phenotypes in screening programs. We are also asking whether this standard is always applied and maintained. To initiate the process of screening is one problem; to maintain it with the appropriate structure in the program is another.

A serious gap often exists between potential and achievement of a particular genetic screening program. The fault usually lies in the organization of the program. The medical objective of genetic screening is to reduce the burden and cost of genetic disease. To achieve this goal, a series of structures is required to maintain several interdependent processes for: screening itself; patient retrieval; diagnosis; counseling, and treatment if indicated.

The structure for screening should maintain high specificity and high sensitivity. Each program must establish its own frequency distributions of quantitative phenotypes. Reduction of inter-laboratory variation will improve specificity and sensitivity. This lesson was learned in PKU screening (15). Centralization of the laboratory component and standardization of techniques improves screening efficiency, and this structural concept has been applied to advantage in Tay-Sachs carrier screening.

Specific processes for retrieval of screenees with positive tests, followed by diagnosis and counseling also require specific structures. Uncoupling of the screening process from follow-up was responsible for some of the past failures of screening.

Education of Advocates and Clients

Earlier in this discussion I mentioned that few of us, are aware of our own extensive heterozygosity, or of the special risks to health that some heterozygous states can confer upon us. We have had no educational experience to believe otherwise. Accordingly when the screening experience recruits us to the fold of so-called blighted persons - we find the experience unpleasant. Screening for the sickle trait revealed how persons, without helpful options such as prenatal diagnosis, were confused by a positive screening test result and felt stigmatized by it. Even the Tay-Sachs screening experience with its clearer options, and the strong health orientation of the community at risk, has repeatedly encountered anxiety and confusion among people who learn for the first time that they are heterozygotes. In this context encounters with high-school students have been helpful and informative.

Students today are taught as a matter of course the received doctrine about the physical world; they are not taught biology and genetics, with a corresponding emphasis. There are many reasons for this imbalance in learning but one of them concerns the lack of emphasis we assign to the teachings of Darwin and Mendel and their followers; you do

not have to know their teachings to graduate from high
school. Another concerns the textbooks which determine the
classroom curriculum; even a student who happens to study
biology, will encounter little genetics and less human
genetics in his course work.

My colleagues and I surveyed nine widely used high
school biology texts (16). We found that only 10 percent
of the typical text concerns genetics and only about 20
percent of text material is devoted to human biology. We
examined the genetic material in the two texts in highest
use in our local school system. We found that human
examples were used less than half the time to illustrate
basic themes in genetics. Indeed in the text called Human
Physiology, the chromosomes of the fruit fly are shown
rather than those of man. So much for the problem of human
genetics in biology textbooks - excellent as they are in so
many other ways.

We then surveyed 930 students taking biology in
Montreal schools to evaluate their knowledge and attitudes
(16). The students surveyed represented 44 percent of those
enrolled in the biology curriculum. However because biology
is not compulsory, they constituted only 11 percent of all
students in the school system under survey. Most biology
students have a high preference for those topics in the
biology curriculum that relate to evolution, genetics and
human biology. But these are not the topics that receive
major emphasis in the texts or in the curriculum.

We went on to examine student knowledge of some basic
facts in human genetics. We found to our astonishment,
that half the students are confused about the difference
between chromosomes and genes. Mendel's laws are also
poorly understood and the basic facts of human sex
determination were again not well perceived. It is not
surprizing then that their understanding of heritability
and of widely-publicized genetic diseases was also found to
be shaky.

On the other hand, student attitudes are largely
positive toward genetic issues in society. Students
believe genetic screening is important yet many of them do
not believe that they, as individuals, could be carriers of
potentially harmful genes. The concept of prevalent
heterozygosity with risk is unfamiliar to the majority of
students. A similar survey in the United States carried out
by the Biological Sciences Curriculum Study has corroborated
these findings in a larger sample of students.

This abbreviated summary highlights certain points of interest for this symposium.

First   Future citizens are not systematically educated in the rudiments of their own biological nature.

Second   Students have an interest in human genetics and they hold positive attitudes towards genetics and social issues but there is quite a gap between their interest and the level of their knowledge about the basic facts of heredity.

Third   The available resources such as textbooks do not effectively close the gap.

If our findings describe today's students, then the situation is surely worse for their parents. There is in all likelihood a national illiteracy in genetics. Our findings may explain why citizens are not easily recruited into heterozygote screening programs and do not interpret the test result appropriately when heterozygosity is identified.

I have made a rather oblique contribution to this symposium hoping thereby to make my point more memorable. I could have enumerated the heterozygous states where screening has been attempted or might be imminently feasible. I considered this approach uninteresting. I could have dissected the past experience with Tay-Sachs carrier or sickle cell trait screening but others, including myself have done that elsewhere. It seemed to me that the major issue in the subject of heterozygote screening was the fact of prevalent human heterozygosity. In that context, the exciting studies of dominantly inherited LDL-cholesterol binding deficiency, which are still in progress and are the subject of recent reviews (17), seem to point the way to a larger view of how some cases of so-called common disease may occur.

If disease is a state of disequilibrium, being the unfolding of particular risks in specific persons, early identification of those at risk is our best option for the prevention of disease in them or their offspring. If we accept this argument, then we must use screening tests with the utmost accuracy to classify genotypes. That is why I offered more than one may have desired to know about the problems of classifying quantitative and qualitative phenotypes. But even if the genetic paradigm of disease is valid, and even if screening tests are near perfect, progress will be slow until society believes in the fact of prevalent heterozygosity, its significance and the option for preventive medicine inherent in the awareness. That is why I see a need for better general education in human genetics. Copernicus' day came long ago in our education. The messages of Darwin and Mendel have yet to be heard clearly in most high schools, classrooms and clinics - and in Congress where the National Genetic Diseases Act of 1976 (PL94-278) languishes near unto death.

References and Notes

1. Juvenal, The Sixteen Satires. Translated with Intro. and notes by Peter Green. Penguin Books, 1967.

2. V.A. McKusick, Mendelian Inheritance in man. Catalogs of autosomal dominant, autosomal recessive and X-linked phenotypes. Johns Hopkins Univ. Press, Baltimore, 4th edit., 1975.

3. B. Childs and V.M. Der Kaloustian, Genetic Heterogeneity. New Engl. J. Med. 279, 1205 and 1267 (1968).

4. C.R. Scriver, Human Biochemical Genetics. A view on individuality. Excerpta Med. ICS 411. Human Genetics. Proc. 5th Int. Cong. Human Genetics, Excerpta Medica, Amsterdam p. 142, 1977.

5. D.A. Hopkinson, N. Spencer and H. Harris, Genetical studies on human red cell acid phosphatase. Ann. Hum. Genet. 16, 141 (1964).

6. H. Harris and D.A. Hopkinson, Average heterozygosity per locus in man: an estimate based on the incidence of enzyme polymorphisms. Ann. Hum. Genet. 36, 9 (1972).

7. H. Harris, Enzyme variants in human populations. The Johns Hopkins Med. J. 138, 245 (1976).

8. B. Culliton, Sickle cell anemia: The route from obscurity to prominence. Science 178, 138 (1972).

9. Comm. for the Study of Inborn Errors of Metabolism. National Research Council. Genetic Screening. Programs, Principles and Research. Nat. Acad. of Sciences, Washington, D.C. 1976.

10. J.M.G. Wilson and G. Jungner. Principles and practice of screening for disease. Public Health Papers #34, World Health Organization, Geneva, 1968.

11. U.R. Maag and R.J.M. Gold, A simple combinatorial method for calculating genetic risks. Clin. Genet. 7, 361 (1975).

12. M. Zannis-Hadjopoulos, R.J.M. Gold, U.R. Maag, J.D. Metrakos and C.R. Scriver, Improved detection of β-thalassemia carriers by a two-test method. Hum. Genet. 38, 315 (1977).

13. E.A. Murphy and G.A. Chase, Principles of Genetic Counseling, Year Book Medical Pub., Chicago, 1975.

14. R.J.M. Gold, U.R. Maag, J.L. Neal and C.R. Scriver, The use of biochemical data in screening for mutant alleles and in genetic counselling. Ann. Hum. Genet. 37, 315 (1974).

15. C.R. Scriver, Screening, Counseling and Treatment for Phenylketonuria: Lessons Learned -- A Précis. In H.A. Lubs and F. de la Cruz, eds. Genetic Counseling, Raven Press, New York, 253, 1977.

16. C.R. Scriver, D.E. Scriver, C. Clow and M. Schok, The education of citizens: Human genetics. Amer. Biol. Teacher 40, 280 (1978).

17. J.L. Goldstein and M.S. Brown, The LDL cholesterol pathway. Ann. Rev. Biochem. 46, 897 (1977).

Acknowledgements

Work and discussion with Barton Childs, Carol Clow, Reynold Gold and Claude Laberge, among others, are the roots of this paper. I am grateful to the Medical Research Council of Canada and the Ministry of Social Affairs (P.Q.) (Quebec Network of Genetic Medicine) and the McGill University-Montreal Children's Hospital Research Institute for their support.

3

Screening of Newborn Infants

Robert Guthrie

Introduction

Phenylketonuria (PKU) was discovered by Fölling in Norway in 1934, as an abnormally high concentration of urine phenylpyruvic acid, or phenylketone, inherited from both parents by Mendelian inheritance with a 1/4 chance of occurrence in each offspring(1). Soon afterward, Jervis showed that the abnormality was due to lack of a single enzyme that converted the essential amino acid, phenylalanine, by a simple hydroxylation step, into the amino acid, tyrosine. In 1939, Block described a simple method for removing phenylalanine from a protein digest and suggested this as a basis for a low phenylalanine diet treatment. In 1953, Bickel demonstrated that such a diet produced a dramatic normalization of behavior in a hyperactive young child with PKU(2). During the next 15 years, this dietary method was applied to many young PKU children to prevent further damage to brain development. Successful effects, however, were only obtained in very young infants discovered by a blood phenylalanine test, performed because an older sibling, already severely retarded, had previously been diagnosed as having PKU.

In the mid 1950's, Dr. Willard Centerwall pushed for urine screening of infants' wet diapers with the $FeCl_3$* test for PKU. Large programs were organized in various countries; but results were very disappointing, although some infants were discovered and treatment started within the first year of life.

Obviously, what was needed was a reliable but economical test for blood phenylalanine. We were fortunate enough to develop such a test, using dried blood spots on filter paper, in 1961(3). By coincidence, that year the National Associa-

---

*$FeCl_3$ = Ferric chloride

Figure 1. NARC Poster Children

tion for Retarded Children (NARC) - as it was then named - used as its "poster child" two children (Fig. 1) - sisters with PKU - showing prevention of retardation in the younger sister due to diet treatment, to emphasize that retardation could sometimes be prevented, and also the need for more research into causes and prevention. I was an NARC research grantee at that time, and willingly cooperated in the NARC's use of my work, and the PKU test, in their publicity. The NARC, through its many state chapters, was successful in getting state laws passed requiring PKU testing, so that by 1967 nearly 40 states had such laws. With the notable exception of Massachusetts, these laws were passed in spite of lack of support, and often active opposition, of the states' medical societies. As a result, by 1970 the U.S. Maternal and Child Health Service found that 90% of infants in the United States were being tested for PKU. In a few states without these laws, only approximately 50% of the infants are screened, even at present.

Multiple Tests and Regionalization

With the dried blood spot specimen and the principle of the bacterial inhibition assay, we developed four more tests by 1967 which were immediately put to trial by four collaborating laboratories, as an organized effort supported initially by the U.S. Children's Bureau and the Maternal and Child Health Service within the H.E.W. These laboratories covered Massachusetts, Oregon, portions of Los Angeles, and Western New York*. Their use of this battery of tests was facilitated by a "punch index" machine (Fig. 2) which automated use of the dried blood spots. However, in the U.S., the PKU specimen was not used for other tests outside of these four laboratories. In other countries with national health care systems, results were much more encouraging. The PKU test was adopted rather quickly in most of these countries, with no need for laws. In many countries, our other tests were added to the PKU test during the late 1960's with active assistance from us in training laboratory personnel and supplying some starting materials.

In 1968-69, during my sabbatical year in New Zealand, a Pacific multiple test program was established** for ten Pacific Island groups who sent their infant dried blood specimens by air mail to the New Zealand laboratory(4).

In 1971, we began a series of three small annual conferences in Buffalo to interest other states and Canadian

*The directors of these laboratories were Dr. R. A. MacCready, Mr. G. Brandon, Dr. R. Straus, and Dr. J. Puleo
**by Prof. A. M. O. Veale

Figure 2. Punch-Index Machine (1967 Model)

provinces in the addition of other tests to their PKU programs. At these conferences, the directors of our collaborating laboratories testified that the use of the punch-index
machine had allowed them to add tests for galactosemia, homocystinuria, maple syrup urine disease, tyrosinemia, and histidinemia* with only marginal increases in costs, since no
additional laboratory staff was required. As a result,
Maryland and Ohio added other tests. New York State applied
the Western New York program to the rest of the state. However, for most states, the legacy of the 1960's controvery
concerning PKU remained in the 1970's in the form of three
problems:

(1) Lack of liaison between the medical centers and
    the screening programs: Even well organized
    regional screening programs located in state
    health departments often had little or no contact
    with medical centers with resulting problems in
    medical follow-up. This is in complete contrast
    to all other countries where the screening labora-
    tory, often for an entire country (as in Austria
    or the Republic of Ireland, for example) is usu-
    ally located in the pediatric department of a uni-
    versity medical school.

(2) Many states with laws requiring PKU testing simply
    do not have sufficient population to make multiple
    testing of newborn infants practical.

(3) Many states with large populations allow private
    laboratories to each perform a small number of
    PKU tests for a profit, thus causing the same
    problem that exists in the small states.

In 1972(7), we published a paper on this subject, calling on the existing state PKU programs to reorganize into
cost-effective regions, suggesting that low-populated states
could cooperate with each other. We discussed this possibility with the Maternal and Child Health Service, with our
collaborating laboratories, and with appropriate persons in
a number of other states where we showed a film prepared

---

*Editors' Note: While in all the disease entities mentioned
early screening and treatment is necessary, this is not true
for histidinemia which has been found to be a "benign" amino
acid disorder. However, all the necessary data with respect
to histidinemia is not yet available. Thus, as a result of
mass screening, new information of the latent clinical and
biochemical natures of many of these disorders might be
forthcoming(5,6).

for this purpose. Meanwhile, a very significant development
was occurring in the Quebec province that proved of great
assistance to this effort(8).

The Quebec genetic network has the features of the
European countries in that the screening center is located
in a university medical center, with the program directed by
the four universities and funding supplied by the Ministry
of Health. A unique feature is that the Government supplies
an extra 50% of funding for research and development of new
genetic services. This made possible during 1971-75 a successful field trial of Dr. Jean Dussault's new radioimmunoassay for hypothyroidism on the dried blood specimen collected for PKU testing. Since every physician knows of the
treatment of hypothyroidism by thyroxine to prevent cretinism and mental retardation, the success of the Quebec program aroused intense interest elsewhere.

In 1975, Dr. William Murphey first introduced the thyroxine test into the U.S. in the Oregon Health Department,
using a minor modification of the punch-index machine to
integrate this test into the Oregon State program (9). As a
result, the states of Montana, Alaska, Idaho, and Nevada made
arrangements to send their specimens to Oregon. In 1976, the
New England region was established after Drs. Levy and
Mitchell added the thyroxine test to the Massachusetts program, with Maine, Rhode Island, Connecticut, and New
Hampshire sending their specimens to the Boston laboratory
(10).

Maryland, Ohio, and New York states have also added thyroxine testing, but for most other states, the fragmented
nature of PKU screening has prevented addition of this test
because of the high cost.

Results of screening so far have demonstrated that the
frequency of hypothyroidism is approximately 1/5,000 or more
than double that of PKU, which has a frequency anywhere from
1/10,000-1/100,000* and that none of these infants would
have been detected during the first three months of life
without the screening test, even when born in the most
sophisticated academic medical center. Thyroxine treatment
is much simpler than treatment for PKU, and screening for
hypothyroidism is even more cost-effective.

Mass Screening for the Hemoglobinopathies

A practical electrophoresis method of using the newborn

*1/8,000 in Europe, but only 1/100,000 in Japan.

dried blood spot specimen in mass screening for sickle cell
hemoglobin and other hemoglobin variants has been developed
by Dr. Michael Garrick in our laboratory(11). A follow-up
procedure using agar electrophoresis on the same blood spot
can differentiate the SA heterozygote from the SS homozygote.
Using this procedure, filter paper specimen for the PKU test
can be screened by a laboratory already performing multiple
tests on the specimens at a material cost of $0.03 per speci-
men. The capital investment for equipment is less than
$1,000 to acquire the capability for screening up to 100,000
specimens per year. In New York state, every newborn infant
has been tested with this procedure for the past two years.
This experience should lead to use of this test by other
screening programs in the immediate future(12).*

In the United States, the Federal Government, through
H.E.W., should provide leadership and enough financial aid
to encourage the other states to follow the example of
Massachusetts and Oregon in establishing cost-effective
screening regions(13).

The Center for Disease Control could be encouraged to
give valuable assistance in providing training programs and
quality control, as it has so effectively in the past for
other laboratory health programs.

In Canada, the provinces outside of Quebec also need to
act. For example, the four Western provinces could logically
form a single screening region.

Future Possibilities

What are some future possibilities of newborn screening?
The prenatal blood specimen, used in Oregon, is already collected everywhere for serology. The alpha-fetoprotein test
of maternal blood serum to detect neural tube defects, already routinely used in Great Britain (See Milunsky Chapter)
will inevitably be used here and elsewhere and should be

*Editors' Note: Although some still question the value of
screening for sickle cell disease, in our opinion there are
two advantages for doing this:
1) diagnosing sickle cell disease at birth is important
in order that the parents be alerted to the nature of this
disease to assure that the infant becomes part of an adequate
health delivery system early in life, and
2) early diagnosis of the disease may be followed by
effective genetic counseling and prenatal diagnosis in subsequent pregnancies, which, though still experimental, is
now available (See Nathan Chapter in this volume).

incorporated into the regional newborn center's program for
greatest efficiency. There is no reason these tests, including the serological ones, can't be adapted to a dried
blood spot for greater efficiency.

The cord blood filter paper specimen, now collected
routinely only in Massachusetts, when used for galactosemia
screening, saves three or four days' time that can be life-
saving as 25-30% of these infants can die within 10 days
when untreated, often with overwhelming E. coli sepsis, as
recently documented by Levy(14). In addition, the real possibility is imminent of a practical screening test for the
Type II heterozygote for familial hypercholesterolemia, or
hyperbetalipoproteinemia, for which a growing body of opinion
suggests early treatment may add 10-20 years of healthy adult
life by prevention of artherosclerosis(15,16).

Urine impregnated filter paper is collected routinely
at 2-4 weeks of age by the infants' mothers in five programs
in Sydney and Perth, Australia; Massachusetts; Quebec; and
British Columbia. These programs have detected approximately
20 additional metabolic abnormalities, mostly very rare, by
paper and thin-layer chromatography and spot tests. We are
currently evaluating an alternative battery of bacterial
tests used with the punch-index machine, in the hope of re-
ducing costs. Among the important conditions detectable are
cystinuria (easily treated by increased water intake to prevent kidney damage by cystine stone formation) and several
different urea cycle defects that can be treated by protein
restriction or the more recent use of the keto acids of the
essential amino acids to reduce blood ammonia levels associated with these inborn errors. Probably, one of the most
important conditions to detect is methylmalonic aciduria,
especially the type treatable by Vitamin B_{12}.

These urine specimens also serve as important follow-up
tests for PKU, homocystinuria, histidinemia, and the various
types of tyrosinemia, necessary because of the early age of
collection of the nursery blood spots due to early hospital
discharge.

Fifteen years ago, most PKU programs collected second
blood specimens at one month, but this was later discontinued
except in Oregon and Los Angeles. Connecticut and Maryland
programs have now reinstituted collection of the four-week
blood specimen, because of concern that PKU cases will be
missed due to early hospital discharge. Moreover, this specimen is probably optimal for detection of homocystinuria,
histidinemia, and the severe form of transient neonatal
tyrosinemia. The latter condition occurs at a frequency of

1/2,000 in countries like ours where artificial infant feed-
ing is the norm, and is treated simply with Vitamin C supple-
mentation, and lowering the excessive protein intake to a
reasonable level. Further, this specimen can be used for a
repeat T_4 test for hypothyroidism, as is done routinely in
Oregon and Maryland programs, where already at least one case
was detected by this means that would have been missed.

A very exciting recent possibility lies in the new
radioimmunoassay on a dried blood spot for congenital adreno-
hyperplasia. The real frequency of this condition is unknown
but lack of early detection and treatment is a real tragedy
to the child, so that pilot programs are certainly indicated
(17).

Finally, to return to the present situation, what can
we recommend immediately for better use of the filter paper
blood specimens already collected from virtually every infant born?

First, the General Accounting Office of the United
States, in their comprehensive report to Congress dated
October 7, 1977(18), in Chapter 3, states that screening all
U.S. infants with seven of these tests and treating all cases
found would cost $18 million annually, but would save at
least $400 million annually in costs of care without detec-
tion and treatment (Table 1). We agree with the GAO as does
Benjamin Franklin in his famous statement on "an ounce of
prevention".

Four important aspects, other than screening, must be
emphasized:

(1) <u>Clinical follow-up treatment</u> has to be planned
    simultaneously with the screening program. This
    requires involvement of the pediatric centers
    from the beginning.

(2) <u>The community</u> to be screened must be fully in-
    formed and the professional community educated.

(3) <u>An advisory committee</u> for the regional program
    should be created to represent the public and
    professional community.

(4) As in Quebec, Massachusetts, Oregon, and elsewhere,
    the screening program should be used as a <u>resource</u>
    for developing new screening services through
    research and trial of new methods. This purpose
    will also require close relations with academic
    medical centers.

Table 1.   Comparison of cost of screening and

Disorder	Projected annual occurrence (note a)	Screening (note b)	Estimated cost of screening and treatment	
			Lifetime treatment cost	
			Undiscounted estimate	Present value (note d)
Phenylketonuria	273	$2,363,000	$ 983,000	$ 749,000
Maple Syrup Urine Disease	15	473,000	3,750,000	781,000
Homocystinuria	14	473,000	1,092,000	176,000
Galactosemia	42	473,000	(c)	(c)
Tyrosinosis	10	473,000	1,500,000	495,000
Histidinemia	131	473,000	(c)	(c)
Hypothyroidism	630	1,575,000	4,914,000	792,000
Total cost for screening		$6,303,000	6,303,000	6,016,000
Total cost of screening and treatment			$18,542,000	$9,009,000
Total lifetime care cost				

treatment and savings of lifetime care costs*

| | | Estimated savings of lifetime care costs | |
| Estimated percentage retarded in absence of screening | Number retarded (note e) | Projected lifetime cost of care | |
		Undiscounted estimate	Present value
99	270	$189,254,000	$35,939,000
5	1	618,000	320,000
75	11	4,177,000	1,378,000
34	14	6,134,000	2,486,000
5	1	528,000	249,000
10	13	10,695,000	1,724,000
42	265	225,779,000	36,398,000
		$437,185,000	$78,494,000

Notes

*From Report to the Congress by the Comptroller General of the United States "Preventing Mental Retardation -- More Can Be Done", October 3, 1977 (HRD-77-37)

(a) Computed by dividing 1974 births (rounded to 3.15 million) by incidence estimates obtained from the National Academy of Sciences and professionals in the field of metabolic disorders.

(b) Based on estimated costs of screening using centralized automated laboratories. Allowance for sample collection is included in cost of PKU screening. All others represent only incremental cost to add them to PKU screening.

(c) Treatment is not considered to incur significant costs above and beyond routine health care.

(d) Costs were discounted at an annual rate of 10 percent.

(e) Column 2 times column 6.

Conclusions

Finally, in urging organization of national newborn
screening programs, let me refer to the present situation
in Japan – a country of 110 million people, half the size
of the U.S. Here, the Japanese Government three years ago
agreed to support a national program as a result of a cam-
paign carried out by a coalition of Japanese pediatricians
and parents' associations for the mentally retarded. The
Kitasato Institute in Tokyo provided a training program for
80 technicians from all over Japan, in which I participated
one year ago, and also assists with quality control. As in
certain other endeavors, Japan started years later than the
U.S., but appears to be already ahead of us. May I close
with the plea that, in newborn screening (if not in cameras
and television sets), we can catch up with Japan!

References

1. Fölling, A. Uber ausschiedung von phenylabrenztrauben-
    sare in den harn als stoffweichselanomalie in ver-
    bindung mit imbezillitat. Hoppe-Seylers Z.
    Physiol. Chem. 227, 169, 1934.

2. Bickel, H., Gerrard, J. and Hickmans, E.M.: Influence
    of phenylalanine intake on phenylketonuria.
    Lancet II, 313, 1953.

3. Guthrie, R.: Blood screening for phenylketonuria.
    JAMA 178, 863, 1961.

4. Houston, I.B. and Veale, A.M.O.: Screening for inborn
    errors of metabolism. Laboratory Management 9,
    30, 1971.

5. Holtzman, N.A.: Newborn screening for genetic-metabolic
    diseases. Progress, principles, and recommenda-
    tions. U. S. Department of Health, Education and
    Welfare. Public Health Service Health Services
    Administration, Bureau of Community Health Services,
    Rockville, Maryland 20857 DHEW, Publication No.
    (HSA) 77-5207, 1977.

6. Levy, H.: Genetic screening. Adv. Human Genet. 4,
    1-104, 1973. Reprinted by the U.S. Department
    of Health, Education and Welfare "Genetic Screening
    for Inborn Errors of Metabolism", DHEW Publication
    No. (HSA) 77-5124, 1977, 106 pages.

7. Guthrie, R. Mass screening for genetic disease.
    Hospital Practice 7, 93, 1972, and from Medical
    Genetics, ed. by McKusick, V. and Claiborne, R.
    HP Publishing Co., Inc., New York, 1973.

8. Cretinism rate spurs regional screening for hypothy-
    roidism. Pediatric News. 10, February, 1976.

9. Cretinism, or hypothyroidism, detection in Oregon.
    Oregon Health Bulletin 53, September, 1975.

10. Brandon, G.R.: Regionalization of public health
    metabolic laboratories. Public Health Laboratories
    34, 56, March, 1976.

11. Garrick, M.D., Dembure, P. and Guthrie, R. Sickle-cell
    anemia and other hemoglobinopathies. Procedures
    and strategy for screening employing spots of

blood on filter paper as specimens. New Engl. J. Med. 288, 1256, 1973.

12. Grover, R., Wethers, D., Shahidi, S., Grossi, M., Goldberg, D., and Davidow, B. Evaluation of the expanded newborn screening program in New York City. Pediatrics 61, 740, 1978.

13. Congressional record, proceedings and debates of the 95th congress, second session 124 (February 28, 1978).

14. Levy, H.L., Sepe, S.J., Shih, V.E., Vawter, G.F. and Klein, J.O.: Sepsis due to Escherichia coli in neonates with galactosemia. New Engl. J. Med. 297, 825, 1977.

15. Drash, A.: Artherosclerosis, cholesterol, and the pediatrician. J. Peds. 80, 693, 1972.

16. Kannel, W.B. and Dawber, T.R.: Artherosclerosis as a pediatrics problem. J. Peds. 80, 544, 1972.

17. Pang, S., Hotchkiss, J., Drash, A.L., Levine, L.S. and New, M.I.: Microfilter paper method for 17 - hydroxyprogesterone radioimmunoassay: its application for rapid screening for congenital adrenal hyperplasia. J. Clin. Endocrinol. Metabolism 45, 1003, 1977.

18. Preventing mental retardation - more can be done. Report to the congress by the comptroller general of the United States. HRD-77-37, 30, October 3, 1977.

4

Screening for Alpha-1-antitrypsin Deficiency

Richard C. Talamo

Introduction

Severe alpha-1-antitrypsin deficiency was first described by Laurell and Eriksson in Sweden fifteen years ago (1) and has become clearly associated with an early onset obstructive lung disease (panacinar emphysema) in childhood or young adult life and/or serious liver disease in infancy, childhood or adult life (2). Approximately 80% of individuals born with severe alpha-1-antitrypsin deficiency will develop early onset emphysema; another 10% will have liver disease beginning in early infancy, resulting in chronic illness or death in many cases; the remainder may remain asymptomatic throughout their lives, but will demonstrate laboratory abnormalities in lung and/or liver function if closely studied.

Genetics

Over 20 codominant alleles have been found to be responsible for the inheritance of serum alpha-1-antitrypsin, with regard to both levels of the protein and electrophoretic mobility (2). A variety of biochemical, immunochemical and electrophoretic techniques is available to quantitate and genetically analyze alpha-1-antitrypsin types (3). This system of alleles is called the Pi (protease inhibitor) system. Normal individuals are of Pi MM* phenotype, those with severe deficiency are called Pi ZZ* and the carriers of the deficiency gene are Pi MZ. Pi Z individuals occur in this country in a frequency of 1/3600 live births, while Pi MZ individuals may comprise as much as 4-5% of the

---

* By international agreement these homozygous individuals are called Pi M and Pi Z, respectively, unless the genetics of their family has been confirmed.

population. Pi Z individuals have a clear susceptibility to the diseases described above, while Pi MZ individuals may possess some increased risk of lung or liver disease, but have no definite tendency toward developing overt clinical disease.

Other factors in addition to the severe alpha-1-antitrypsin deficiency of Pi Z individuals may determine the age of onset and severity of clinical illness. These factors include smoking; the inherited levels of neutrophil enzymes like elastase (4); possibly air pollution and possibly severe pulmonary infection.

Experience in Alpha-1-antitrypsin Screening

Sensitive, inexpensive and specific screening methods are available for detection of Pi Z or Pi MZ alpha-a-antitrypsin deficiency in serum (5). These quantitative determinations can then be confirmed by genetic electro-phoretic analysis of samples from individuals detected in the screening process. Several large screening studies are available in the world experience:

A prospective study of 200,000 newborns using an electroimmunoassay has been reported by Sveger from Sweden (6). One hundred twenty Pi Z infants were detected. The most striking finding was the presence of severe obstructive jaundice in 7% of these infants, with as many as ½ of the rest having biochemical abnormalities suggesting damage to bile ducts or liver. Laboratory evidence of abnormal liver function, in spite of absence of clinical liver disease, was detected for as long as 6 months after birth. This population of deficient individuals will be followed for further development of liver and lung disease.

Several large community surveys have been performed, in an attempt to correlate the Pi MZ phenotype with a history or clinical findings of pulmonary disease. In the largest study, by Morse, et al, in Arizona, in a population of 2,944 subjects there were 88 Pi MZ persons (7). In comparison to the Pi M normals, there was no significant increase in respiratory history or in the laboratory diagnosis of ventilatory impairment, nor any differences in the rate of decrease of pulmonary function with age or smoking in the Pi MZ group. It was concluded that screening of the general population for heterozygous alpha-1-antitrypsin deficiency is not worthwhile.

Several studies are available of selected populations of Pi MZ individuals (8). In general, these studies demonstrated essentially normal pulmonary function in non-smoking Pi MZ individuals, but greater than expected deterioration with age in smoking Pi MZ individuals. In most of these studies, the Pi MZ individuals do not have severe chronic obstructive pulmonary disease, but rather only minimal laboratory evidence of such disease, using very sensitive tests.

A few large population studies of working individuals have been published, in which full pulmonary histories, lung function analysis and alpha-1-antitrypsin Pi typing have been done. For example, in a study of 1,995 working individuals, 35-70 years of age, from many different occupations, Cole, in northern Ireland, found that respiratory symptoms and a history of previous chest illness were of the same frequency in Pi M and Pi MZ individuals (9). Deterioration of lung function with age was similar for both types, even when subgroups were separated by smoking or dust exposure history. It was concluded that Pi MZ individuals are not more than usually liable to develop chronic airways obstruction.

Conclusions

While considerable information has accumulated in a variety of screening programs for alpha-1-antitrypsin deficiency, the true clinical significance of many of the variant phenotypes remains to be discovered. The deleterious effects of industrial pollutants and tobacco smoke have not clearly been demonstrated in Pi MZ individuals (who carry the deficiency gene). At the time of birth it is not yet possible to know whether a severely deficient Pi Z individual will develop early liver disease, or perhaps lung disease beginning in the third decade of life, or never develop any clinical disease syndrome. Further, there is no specific treatment for alpha-1-antitrypsin deficiency at the current time, although there is promise that replacement of this serum protein or provision of a substitute protease inhibitor to deficient individuals will be available in the relatively near future. For these reasons, it would not yet seem appropriate to begin large scale screening programs for alpha-1-antitrypsin deficiency.

References

1. C.B. Laurell and S. Eriksson: The electrophoretic
   alpha-1-globulin pattern of serum in alpha-1-anti-
   trypsin deficiency, Scand. J. Clin. Lab. Invest. 15,
   132 (1963).

2. R.C. Talamo: Emphysema and Alpha-1-antitrypsin
   Deficiency, in: Disorders of the Respiratory Tract in
   Children, E.L. Kendig and V. Chernick, Eds. (W.B.
   Saunders Co., Phila., 1977), p. 593; S. Eriksson:
   Studies in alpha-1-antitrypsin deficiency, Acta Med.
   Scand. 177, 432 (1965); R.C. Talamo: Basic and clinical
   aspects of the alpha-1-antitrypsin, Pediatrics 56,
   21, (1975).

3. R.C. Talamo, R.M. Bruce, C.E. Langley, R.W. Berninger,
   J.A. Pierce, L.J. Brant and D.B. Duncan, in: Alpha-1-
   antitrypsin Laboratory Manual (U.S. Department of
   Health, Education, and Welfare, Public Health Service,
   National Institutes of Health, DHEW Publication No.
   (NIH) 78-1420, 1978).

4. M. Galdston, A. Janoff and A.L. Davis: Familial
   variation of leukocyte lysosomal protease and serum
   alpha-1-antitrypsin as determinants in chronic obstructive pulmonary disease, Am. Rev. Resp. Dis. 107,
   718 (1973).

5. W. Rawlings, Jr., P. Kreiss, D. Levy, B. Cohen, H.
   Menkes, S. Brashears and S. Permutt: Clinical,
   epidemiologic, and pulmonary function studies in alpha-
   1-antitrypsin-deficient subjects of Pi Z type, Am.
   Rev. Resp. Dis. 114, 945 (1976).

6. C. B. Laurell: A screening test for alpha-1-anti-
   trypsin deficiency. Scand. J. Clin. Lab. Invest. 29,
   247 (1972); C. B. Laurell and T. Sveger: Mass screening
   of newborn Swedish infants for alpha-1-antitrypsin
   deficiency, Am. J. Hum. Genet. 27, 213, (1975).

7. T. Sveger: Liver disease in alpha-1-antitrypsin
   deficiency detected by screening of 200,000 infants,
   New Eng. J. Med. 294, 1316 (1976); J.O. Morse, M.D.
   Lebowitz, R.J. Knudson and B. Burrows: Relation of
   protease inhibitor phenotypes to obstructive lung
   diseases in a community, New Eng. J. Med. 296, 1190
   (1977).

8. D.M. Cooper, V. Hoeppner, D. Cox, N. Zamel, A.C. Bryan and H. Levison: Lung function in alpha-1-antitrypsin heterozygotes (Pi type MZ), Am. Rev. Resp. Dis. 110, 708 (1974); C. Larsson, S. Eriksson and H. Dirkson: Smoking and intermediate alpha-1-antitrypsin deficiency and lung function in middle-aged men, Br. Med. J. I, 922 (1977).

9. R.B. Cole, N.C. Nevin, G. Blundell, J.D. Merrett, J.R. McDonald and W.P. Johnston: Relation of alpha-1-antitrypsin phenotype to the performance of pulmonary function tests and to the prevalence of respiratory illness in a working population, Thorax 31, 149, 1976.

Carrier Detection in 5
Duchenne Muscular Dystrophy
and Implications for Genetic
Counseling in X-linked Disease

Marie-Louise E. Lubs, P. Michael Conneally, Kenneth W. Dumars,
Robert M. Greenstein, and W. Angus Muir

Introduction

The Duchenne type of muscular dystrophy (DMD) is the
most common of the childhood dystrophies. It is caused by an
X-linked recessive gene and affects about one in 5,000 boys.
The muscle deterioration starts at birth or, as indicated by
Dr. Mahoney's work[1], even before birth. The child seems
normal at birth, however, and the clinical symptoms are not
generally detected until one to three years of age, although
in retrospect many of the affected boys have delayed gross
motor milestones. The first symptoms are a waddling gait,
difficulty in climbing stairs and hypertrophy of the calf
muscles. The muscle weakness progresses and the child is
usually wheelchair-bound by the age of eight to ten. Cardio-
myopathy is present in the majority of cases and one third to
one half have some degree of mental retardation. The average
survival age is 17 and 75% die before the age of 20. The
gene for this disorder is inherited on the X chromosome.
Since females have two X chromosomes and males have only one,
genetic selection is present on 1/3 of the genes, those
present in the males. The reproductive fitness for affected
males is zero, meaning that no males survive to reproduce.
Therefore, one third of the genes in the gene pool are lost
in each generation. Since the disease frequency remains
constant from generation to generation, an equal number of
genes are added to the gene pool by means of new mutations.
For genetic counseling purposes, the comparatively large
proportion (about one third) of cases which are due to new
mutations is very important. In about half the cases, a
positive family history can be obtained which would identify
the mother as being a carrier. Among the other half of the
cases, however, some represent a new mutation in the child,
which means that the recurrence risk for parents is virtually
zero. In other families, the mother represents the new

mutation or in a few instances the gene has been inherited in
several generations and by chance only females and no males
have inherited it. If the mother is a carrier, the recurrence risk is one in four or 25% which, given the high burden
of the disease, most couples consider to be a very high risk
Therefore, it becomes very important among those cases with
a negative family history, to establish whether the mother is
a carrier or the son represents a new mutation.

CPK Levels and the Diagnosis of Duchenne Muscular Dystrophy

One of the characteristic features that is used to diag-
nostically differentiate between Duchenne muscular dystrophy
and other types of childhood dystrophies is a grossly elevated level of creatine phosphokinase (CPK) in the blood serum.
Some CPK is released from the muscle cells into the blood-
stream in normal muscle, and the abnormally high levels in
patients with DMD may be due to a defect in the muscle cell
membrane. In our laboratory, normal males usually have a CPK
level under 150 International Units per liter (IC/l). In
young boys with DMD, the levels are often several thousand
IU/l. During the later stages of the disease, when all the
muscle fibers have deteriorated, the CPK levels decrease,
sometimes down to normal levels.

Carrier Detection

The level of CPK in serum is also used to determine the
carrier state in females. As with most carrier tests for X-
linked disorders, it is not a very exact one, since many carriers test within normal limits. This is due to a phenomenon
called lyonization (after Mary Lyon, who first described it
in 1961[2]), which takes place early in fetal life of females,
possibly at the late blastocyst stage. Lyonization is the
random inactivation of one X chromosome in each cell of the
fetus, with the possible exception of the ovarian cells.[3]
On the average, therefore, females have one half of their
cells with their maternal X chromosome active and one half
with their paternal X chromosome being the functioning one.
If the maternal X chromosome contains a gene for Duchenne
muscular dystrophy, about one half of the muscle cells will
have the membrane defect which leads to elevated CPK levels
in the blood serum. However, since the number of cells that
will develop to muscles are comparatively few at the late
blastocyst stage, it is possible that by chance a significant
ly larger proportion then 50% of the activated X chromosomes in these cells will be paternal. In those cases, the
elevation of CPK may be very slight or, in fact, CPK levels
may be normal. Regardless of the X chromosome distribution

in the muscle cells, however, the ovaries will produce ova
in equal number with the maternal and paternal X chromosome,
respectively. Therefore, even though a female carrier may
have normal CPK levels, her chance of transmitting the gene
to her offspring is still one in two or 50%.

The problem with lyonization is present in most X-linked
diseases in which the product measured is not the primary
gene product. The elevated CPK, for instance, or the clotting activity in the blood (which can be an indication of the
carrier state in hemophilia) are very indirect indications of
the gene activity. Only by cloning single cells and measuring the presence or absence of the primary gene activity is
it possible to detect whether there are two types of cells
present, those with a normal gene and those with an abnormal
one.

Although there are other carrier tests for Duchenne
muscular dystrophy, particularly some involving muscle biopsy
and examining the histological and biochemical properties
of the muscle fibers, they all have the limitation that at
least 15% of carriers test within the 95% limit of normal
controls. Since the carrier frequency is approximately 1 in
2,500 females, this would mean that one would falsely identify 147 normal women as carriers for each actual carrier
identified. There is a type of limited screening, however,
that would be helpful. Fifty percent of affected boys are
born to women who had an affected relative, usually brother
or maternal uncle already diagnosed at the time of conception
of the affected son. Therefore, by obtaining a family
history prior to the pregnancy, a family doctor or an OB-GYN
specialist can identify the woman as being at risk of being
a carrier. These women can then be carrier tested and with a
much higher probability of being correctly identified as
carriers. Unfortunately, this is very rarely done.

A different approach has been used in Colorado. We have
ascertained a large number of females at risk by taking a
family history from all patients in the Muscular Dystrophy
Clinic. Those relatives who had a high risk of being a carrier were then contacted by a geneticist, and asked if they
wanted to come in for carrier testing and genetic counseling.
If the relatives lived outside Colorado, the same information
was given by mail. Of the high risk individuals thus contacted, 39% had not had an affected child and the majority of
those were unaware of their increased risk. We call this type
of genetic counseling prospective because of its potential of
reaching high risk individuals before they have children.

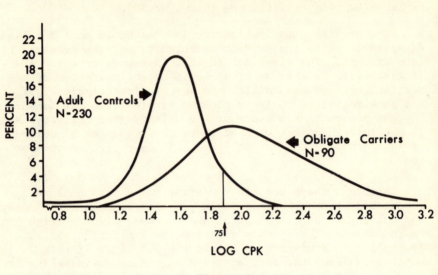

Figure 1

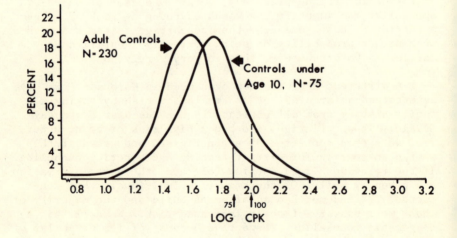

Figure 2

Due to the overlap in CPK levels in normal females and
carriers, it is possible to give only a relative risk based
on the family history and carrier test results.
Figure 1 shows the CPK distribution in adult carriers and
normal controls. The CPK levels are expressed in log values
since this transformation seems to produce normal distributions. The 90% upper limit of normal was found to be 1.88,
which corresponds to a value of 76 IU/1. Figure 2 shows the
distributions in normal prepubertal children and normal females over the age of 15. There was no regression on age before puberty or in the group older than 15. Therefore, the
data suggests that puberty itself, possibly the hormonal
changes at that time, would lower the CPK levels. Supporting
data to this hypothesis include our own and other studies
showing that CPK levels decrease significantly during pregnancy[4], which is also a state with altered sex hormone levels.
Some preliminary data of our own indicate that very young
(prepubertal) carriers may have particularly high CPK levels.
This is somewhat difficult to establish, since a carrier cannot be identified with certainty until she has had an affected child. Through a collaborative effort, however, we have
ascertained a large number of prepubertal girls who all had
a 50% a priori risk of being carriers, i.e., they were daugh-
ters of women who had been identified as obligate carriers.
(Any woman who has an affected son and also another male
relative such as a brother or an uncle affected is considered
to be an obligate carrier). In this group of children, we
were evaluating whether a bimodal distribution of CPK values
could be obtained and if the modes seemed to be better
separated than in a sample from adult carriers and controls.
The practical implications would be that at risk families
should be encouraged to have the girls carrier tested early
rather than at the time of child bearing. Table 1 shows the
average CPK levels by age in individuals at 50% risk of being
carriers. The table shows that as in controls, prepubertal
girls test somewhat higher. In the other age groups, there
seem to be no trend with increasing age.

There may be other indications of the carrier state.
The muscle fibers in affected males have characteristic
staining and other histological properties for instance. A
muscle biopsy can, therefore, give additional information.
Unfortunately, an abnormal biopsy and elevated CPK levels are
highly correlated - the biopsy is rarely abnormal if the CPK
is normal. Since a muscle biopsy is a more involved and expensive procedure than obtaining a venous blood sample, the
latter is normally the preferred method. There are other
methods, such as the determination of the rate of ribosomal
protein synthesis in the muscle fiber.[5] The rate of total

TABLE 1

Mean CPK in females with a 50% prior risk[1] of
being carriers for Duchenne Muscular dystrophy

Age group	No. tested	Mean log CPK	Value IU/1
0-10	19	2.12	131
11-20	28	1.89	78
21-30	40	1.85	71
31-40	11	1.87	74
41+	7	2.32	209

[1]Daughters of obligate carriers. Mothers of probands excluded.

polyribosomal protein synthesis was found by one laboratory to be elevated in affected males and in carrier females. The investigators reported the rate of synthesis was unrelated to the CPK level. This test may prove to be a valuable additional tool to be used in possible carriers, whose CPK is in the normal range. Unfortunately, it is a very expensive and time consuming test and is presently only carried out by Dr. Ionasescu and his group at the University of Iowa.

Clinical Indications of Carrier State

As part of the collaborative efforts, we have looked into some clinical variables that might be indicative of the carrier state. Preliminary data from Colorado showed that there seemed to be no difference between carriers and controls in subjective symptoms such as pain in the legs, hard calves, leg cramps, difficulties in walking stairs or getting up from the floor. However, 45% of carriers thought that they had large calves as opposed to 21% of the controls and 15% thought their calves were unequal in size, as opposed to 7% of controls.6 Therefore, information about height, weight and calf circumference was obtained from an additional sample of 35 obligate carriers. The results are shown in Table 2. The age group 29-35 was selected to minimize environmental variables that may influence these measurements. The table shows that there is very little difference in the three groups. Certainly, from a clinical standpoint, the variables could not be used to improve the prediction that a particular woman is or is not a carrier.

The level of serum CPK is related to physical activity or physical fitness. Normal individuals with better developed muscles are said to have higher CPK levels.[7] Therefore, we obtained the information from each of the obligate carriers whether they thought that they did more or less exercise or physically strenuous work than the average person. The results are shown in relation to CPK levels in Table 3. The table shows that physical fitness does not seem to influence CPK levels in carriers.

Therefore, one is left with only two factors influencing the prediction of the carrier state: The family history and an incompletely discriminatory carrier test. If the family history alone cannot identify a female as being an obligate carrier, one is then left with a probability of being a carrier which varies anywhere from 0 to 100%. A simple example is this: A woman (the consultand) has a brother and a maternal uncle with muscular dystrophy. She has no children. The pedigree is shown in Figure 3. The consultand's mother is an obligate carrier. The consultand has, therefore, an a priori risk of 1/2 to have inherited the gene from her mother. Let us suppose that her log CPK level was found to be 1.6. Six percent of carriers and 19.2% of normal individuals have a level of 1.6, as shown in Figure 2. The calculations of the final risks are shown in Table 4. The probability that two or more independent events occur together is the product of the individual probabilities. This is called the joint probability. In this example, the joint probability is the product of the prior and the conditional probabilities. However, the joint probabilities in the left and the right columns do not add up to unity or 100% and yet, these are the only two possibilities (i.e. the individual in this example is or is not a carrier). Therefore, one must make the two joint probabilities add up to unity or 100% without changing their relative values. This is done by putting the values over a common denominator which is the sum of the individual joint probabilities. This is shown as the posterior probabilities. The final or posterior probability for this woman is 24% of having inherited the gene from her mother and thus being a carrier. There is an additional probability that she did not inherit the gene but is a carrier as a result of a new mutation. This risk, however, is negligible in comparison with the 24% risk of having inherited the gene, and for practical purposes it is not necessary to consider the mutation rate when the family history is positive. If this woman has a normal son, it would decrease her relative probability of being a carrier. If she has a daughter, the CPK level of the daughter would influence not only the risk of the child being a carrier, but also the risk of the mother. Therefore, these calculations can become very complicated at times.

Table 2. Average Measurements in Carriers of the Gene for
Duchenne Muscular Dystrophy and Controls

	Average Measurements		
	Obligate Carriers 29-35 yrs.	Possible Carriers 29-35 yrs.	Controls 29-35 yrs.
Height (cm)	163.07	166.12	160.76
Weight (kg)	63.07	53.39	53.90
Smaller Calf (cm)	33.98	33.91	33.66
Larger Calf (cm)	34.55	34.28	34.30
Average Difference in Calf Size (cm)	.57	.82	.64

Table 3. CPK Levels in Obligate Carriers in Relation to
Physical Fitness

	Exercise More Than Average N=23	Do Not Exercise N=48
Average Log CPK Level	2.05	2.06
Proportion with Log CPK Level > 2.20	26%	35%

FIGURE 3:   EXAMPLE OF A PEDIGREE

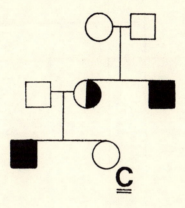

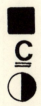 Male with Duchenne muscular dystrophy

Consultand

Obligate carrier

TABLE 4

Relative Risk of Being a Carrier for Duchenne Muscular Dystrophy

(Consultand is a daughter of an obligate carrier; her log CPK level is 1.6)

Probability	Consultand is a Carrier	Consultand is not a Carrier
Prior	0.5	0.5
Conditional: carrier test results	0.060[1]	0.192[1]
Joint	0.5 × 0.060 = 0.030	0.5 × 0.192 = 0.096
Posterior (Final)	$\dfrac{0.03}{0.03 + 0.096} = 0.24$	$\dfrac{0.096}{0.03 + 0.096} = 0.76$

[1]Probabilities obtained from Figure 1

However, it is very important that they be done, since the risk figure does influence the reproductive behavior of individuals at risk. Among individuals at risk of having a child with DMD questioned in Colorado, for instance, 49% thought that the risk of having an affected child of 25% (the risk an obligate carrier would have) is too high to take, whereas only 11% thought a risk of 5% too high to take.

Conclusions

In summary: Most carrier tests for X-linked recessive disorders are of limited value because of the overlap between carriers and controls caused by lyonization. However, the test results can be used in conjunction with information about family history to assess a relative risk for an individual woman of being a carrier. Such relative risk figures are of great value for the family planning for couples at risk.

ADDENDUM: Since this presentation was given, a new carrier test for Duchenne muscular dystrophy has been described by Pickard el al.[8] They found that affected males as well as carrier females have decreased frequency of "capped" lymphocytes (immunofluorescent visualization of aggregation of antigen-antibody complexes on the surface of the cells). Although the numbers of individuals reported were small (42 carriers and 86 controls) the data presented indicate that this method shows less overlap between carriers and controls than other methods presently in use. Thus 7 carriers (17%) tested in the normal range, whereas no normal controls were reported to have decreased frequency of capped lymphocytes. There was no correlation between CPK levels and frequency of capped cells. Therefore, the frequency of capping plus the CPK level together may make it possible to better predict the carrier state. Further studies are needed to confirm these findings.

Editors' Note: Percy, et. al., in 1978(9) reported that the use in combination of measurements of serum hemopexin, CPK, pyruvate kinase and lactic dehydrogenase greatly improved the efficiency of carrier detection for Duchenne Muscular Dystrophy to close to 100%.

62   *Lubs et al.*

References

1.   Mahoney, M., Haseltine, F., Hobbins, J., Barker, B.,
     Caskey, C., and Golbus, M.: Prenatal diagnosis of Duch-
     enne's muscular dystrophy. New England J. Med. 269,
     986-973, 1977.

2.   Lyon, M.F.: Gene action in the X-chromosome of the mouse
     (Mus musculus L.) Nature 190, 372-373, 1961.

3.   Migeon, B.R. and Jelalian, K.: Evidence for two active
     X chromosomes in germ cell of female before meiotic entry
     Nature, 269, 242-243, 1977.

4.   Emery, A.E.H. and King, B.: Pregnancy and serum creat-
     ine kinase levels in potential carriers of Duchenne X-
     linked muscular dystrophy. Lancet 1, 1013, 1977.

5.   Ionasescu, V., Zellweger, H. and Burmeister, L.: Detect-
     ion of carriers and genetic counseling in Duchenne
     muscular dystrophy by ribosomal protein synthesis. Acta
     Neurol. Scand. 54, 442-452, 1976.

6.   Lubs, M.L.E.: Carrier screening in Hemophilia and
     Duchenne muscular dystrophy: economical and psychological
     consequences. In Services and Education in Medical
     Genetics. Eds: I. Porter and E. Hook. Academic Press.
     In press.

7.   Griffiths, D.: Serum levels of ATP: Creatine phospho-
     transferase (creatine kinase). The normal range and
     effects of muscular activity. Clin. Chim. Acta: 13,
     413-420, 1966.

8.   Pickard, N.A., Gruemer, H-D., Verrill, H.L., Isaacs,
     E.R., Robinow, M., Nance, W.E., Myers, E.C., and
     Goldsmith, B.: Systemic membrane defect in the proximal
     muscular dystrophies. N. Engl. J. Med.: 229, 841-846,
     1978.

9.   Percy, M.E., Chang, L., Oss, I., Pitt, M.A., Verellen,
     C., and Thompson, M.W.: An improved method for carrier
     detection in Duchenne Muscular Dystrophy. Abstract,
     The American Society of Human Genetics, 29th Annual
     Meeting, Vancouver, British Columbia, October 4-7, 1978,
     63a.

Part II

Recent Advances and Experience in Prenatal Diagnosis

6

Prenatal Diagnosis
of Chromosomal Disorders

Siegfried M. Pueschel

Prenatal diagnosis of genetic disorders as an important adjunct to clinical medicine had already been
recognized in the beginning of this century and amniocentesis
has been used as a diagnostic tool since the early 1930's
(1,2). During the past two decades transabdominal amniocentesis has gained widespread acceptance since it was found
to be most useful in the management of Rh isoimmunization (3).
Yet, this procedure has become available for diagnosis of a
variety of genetic disorders only in the last 10 years (4).
This paper will focus primarily on chromosomal disorders in
relation to prenatal diagnosis.

The information obtained through amniocentesis and subsequent cell culture has influenced the process of genetic
counseling significantly. Prenatal diagnosis has made it
possible to provide more meaningful information to parents in
many instances. Instead of communicating theoretical risk
figures to parents, prenatal diagnosis can determine whether
a fetus believed to be at risk for a specific genetic disease
actually has that disorder. Couples who previously on the
basis of probability statistics were unwilling to risk a
pregnancy now can have their own children without fearing the
birth of a child with a specific serious genetic disease.
Since in 95% of cases the results of amniocentesis will reveal an unaffected fetus it is important to realize that this
procedure concerns primarily the health and life of children
who might never have been born if this capability did not
exist. Hence, prenatal diagnosis is of enormous positive
human value for many families who have chosen to use it.

Many women who underwent this procedure in our and other amniocentesis programs continued the pregnancy mainly
because of the reassurance they gained from the results (5,6,

65

7). Some of the mothers stated that they would have elected termination of the pregnancy had amniocentesis not been available to them.

If, however, amniotic fluid cell culture should reveal that the fetus has a specific chromosomal anomaly the family may request therapeutic abortion. Should parents not desire to have the pregnancy terminated they then can acclimate to the fact that the child will have a genetic defect and can plan accordingly. In such circumstances physicians never should decide for parents what to do or so influence them that they cannot but agree with the physician's opinion.

It is common practice in our center that both parents are counseled and appropriately informed concerning the procedure prior to amniocentesis. The limitations of the technique involved and the potential hazards are explained in detail. Parents are appraised of the fact that the attempt to obtain amniotic fluid may not be successful. In our experience mothers are likely to be less distressed when they are informed of this possibility in advance. Furthermore, parents are told that occasionally cells obtained from amniotic fluid will not grow sufficiently or th chromosome preparation may be of poor quality and unusable necessitating a second tap. They are informed that a complete and correct diagnosis of the condition of the fetu based on the karyotype cannot be guaranteed and if the chromosome analysis is normal they cannot expect a "perfect baby" since it is known that congenital malformations and mental retardation may arise for reasons totally unrelated to demonstrable karyotypic findings.

As in any medical procedure one also has to expect complications and pitfalls with prenatal diagnosis. The skilled obstetrician performing amniocentesis between the 14th and 16th week of gestation guided by ultrasound techniques and preventing isoimmunization in the Rh-negativ mother usually will not experience any serious problems. The National Institute of Child Health and Human Developmen Collaborative Amniocentesis Registry Project (NICHD) provided evidence of the safety and accuracy of second trimester amniocentesis. During this study immediate complication of amniocentesis including vaginal bleeding or amniotic fluid leakage occurred in only 2% of the women. The rate of spontaneous miscarriage and fetal death of 3.4% was the same in both the study and control groups (6). Similar results were also reported from the Canadian

Collaborative Study where no serious infection or hemorrhage
in mothers were observed and no increased rate of miscar-
riages and fetal loss were recorded (7).

Despite the relative safety of amniocentesis and the
high accuracy rate of over 99%, difficulties arise occasionally when no amniotic fluid is obtained or if suboptimal
cell growth does not allow proper interpretation. Because
of a dry tap in 2-5% of cases a second amniocentesis will
have to be performed and in 5-10% of cases cells from the
amniotic fluid fail to grow in the laboratory culture media
again necessitating a second and sometimes even a third
amniocentesis. Other complications are bloody amniotic fluid
samples, contamination with skin bacteria, and technical or
clerical errors of reporting the results of the chromosomal
analysis. In addition difficulties arise in the interpretation of cytogenetic observations from amniotic fluid
cell cultures in instances of mosaicism, polyploidy,
spontaneous translocations, and subtle chromosomal
abnormalities (10).

Of great concern are erroneous diagnoses. In the NICHD
study five errors of cytogenetic diagnoses occurred whereby
sex was identified incorrectly in three cases, and two
children with Down Syndrome were born despite the initial
report of normal karyotypes. Intensive re-study of these
situations failed to establish causes of the errors (6). In
the Canadian Collaborative Study there were two incorrect
designations of sex (7). Another source of error is the
inability to detect the presence of twins of similar or
possibly even different sex on the basis of chromosomal
analysis. The utilization of sonography prior to amniocentesis, however, will ordinarily identify twin pregnancies.

In our amniocentesis program as well as in other reports
describing similar services the most common indication for
prenatal diagnosis is advanced maternal age (5,6,7,8,9).
While there is no sharp dividing line above which maternal
age is to be considered "advanced", most centers currently
are using 35 years as a criterion, whereas a few years ago
40 years was the designated age. It is a well known fact
that older mothers have an increased risk for giving birth
to a child with a chromosomal aberration. It has been
estimated that the risk for having a chromosomally defective
offspring for women 35 to 39 years of age is slightly more
than 2%, the risk for a women between 40 and 44 years is
3-4%, and for women 45 years or older a 10% risk figure is
provided (8,9).

The second most common indication for prenatal diagnosis is for women who already have a child with Down Syndrome. The literature on this subject provides evidence that the risk of recurrence in this group appears to be 1-2% (6,7,8, 9). In the NICHD study the indication for amniocentesis was advanced maternal age in 47% of cases and a previous child with Down Syndrome was the indication in 26% (6).

Another important indication for amniocentesis relates to chromosomal translocation situations. For example, in Down Syndrome 3-4% of children with this syndrome will have the translocated form. One-half to one-third of these are transmitted by a parent with a balanced translocation. The risk of recurrence depends on what kind of translocation is found and who is carrying the translocation.

While other chromosomal abnormalities are less common indications for amniocentesis, a previous child with Trisomy 13 or Trisomy 18 are also indications for prenatal testing since these parents are assumed to be at a higher risk for having another child with a chromosomal disorder. In the NICHD study further reasons for amniocentesis were a family history of other cytogenetic disorders and parental mosaicism (6).

The determination of X and Y chromosomes has special relevance for disorders inherited as X-linked traits such as hemophilia, Duchenne Muscular Dystrophy, Hunter Syndrome, Lesch-Nyhan Syndrome or Fabry Disease. If a mother is carrying a male fetus the chances are 50% that he may be affected with the respective disorder. Parents may decide in severe X-linked disorders only to have female offspring and not take the risk of the birth of an affected male. Such a couple may exercise the option of having amniocentesis and chromosome determination on the sex of the fetus. They might decide to terminate the pregnancy if the fetus is a male. Since there is a 50% chance that a normal fetus might be aborted, there are increased research efforts in the direction of developing tests to distinguish between affected and unaffected males in X-linked disorders. Such a situation will be discussed by Dr. Mahoney in his paper on prenatal diagnosis of Duchenne Muscular Dystrophy.

As has been noted by other investigators amniocentesis for prenatal diagnosis is markedly underutilized (8,13). According to Rhode Island Vital Statistics approximately 1500 babies were born to mothers in this state 35 years of age or older during a three-year time period (1974-1977),

yet we only received 57 referrals for amniocentesis of women
in this age group. Rhode Island is not unique in this regard. Four percent of older mothers were referred to the
amniocentesis program in Massachusetts and only about two
percent of pregnant women 35 years and older underwent
amniocentesis in California (8,13). These figures have increased recently reaching nearly 25% in some parts of New
York and Georgia (14). It has been estimated that the number of infants born with Down Syndrome probably could be reduced by one-third if amniocentesis would be made available
to all pregnant women 35 years and older.

There are several reasons why amniocentesis is underutilized for patients who are at risk for conditions that
could be diagnosed in utero. Many professionals have felt
that there is an increased risk of the procedure for both
mother and fetus in terms of higher rate of spontaneous
abortions, obstetrical complications, or damages to the
fetus himself.

Yet, the risk of amniocentesis appears to be low based
on cumulative experiences of several genetic centers as well
as the NICHD study (5,6,7). The latter study found no
statistically significant difference between 1040 amniocentesis subjects and 992 control subjects concerning fetal
loss, incidence of complications during pregnancy, or the
occurrence of physical injury to the infant resulting from
amniocentesis (6). The evaluation of our own experience is
in support of these data showing no increase in obstetrical
complications following amniocentesis. We also found that
none of the infants born subsequent to amniocentesis had
any apparent injury or birth defect that may be attributed
to this procedure (5).

Some physicians apparently decline to perform amniocentesis in patients where an anterior placenta is found
by sonography. The analysis of our study, however, provides
evidence that amniocentesis is not associated with an increased obstetrical risk in the presence of an anterior
placenta (5).

More often the reluctance to offer amniocentesis is
based on moral and ethical grounds because of the
association with abortion. We feel that a physician's
personal conviction or viewpoint should not interfere with
accepted practices in medicine. Parents should have access
to prenatal diagnosis if this is indicated and decisions
concerning childbearing should be made only by the couple
involved after being informed of the risks and options.

Because virtually all chromosomal abnormalities can be detected in the fetus today it has been suggested that widescale prenatal screening be made routine medical practice for society if not for individual interests (15). It should be realized that such a strategy would be not only uneconomical, but it would not be feasible with the present laboratory facilities available. The greater the population screened, the lower will be the proportion of fetuses found to be affected. Furthermore, the still undefined upper limit of complications of the procedure would suggest that widescale screening for chromosomal disorders is not indicated at this time.

Beyond the medical aspects there are a number of other factors to be considered in the application of prenatal diagnosis, such as legal, ethical, and moral questions. While selective abortions of fetuses with serious genetic diseases can be debated ethically, questions arise in regard to the rights of the fetus. It has been argued that no one represents the fetus in such decisions.

Other questions are being asked: Will society's tolerance for imperfections become less and less as our methodology to detect imperfection improves? or, As we learn to live with certain genetic diseases, as we succeed in better managing of those disorders, and as new treatment programs become available, will prenatal diagnosis become a mere academic exercise?

While some centers and clinicians make a commitment to abortion a prerequisite for prenatal diagnosis if the fetus is found to be affected, we do not agree with this approach. In our investigations concerning the decision making process in regard to abortion subsequent to positive amniocentesis results we found that parents often have different views after the procedure is done or after the diagnosis has been established compared to their views prior to amniocentesis (16).

In our study prospective parents referred to the disorder's severity as a crucial determinant in selective abortion decision. The more serious the genetic disorder the more likely parents were ready to decide for abortion. Another important element that would influence many parents decision concerned the specific disorder at risk. In addition there were multiple subjective factors including certain preconceptions both of the disease itself and of what such disease would entail for family members. Some parents based their selective abortion decision solely on the interest of the fetus while others considered the existent family's best interest in making their decision. None of the parents, however, based the abortion decisions upon the ill-effect an affected child might have on society.

We found that no one factor was the sole determinant in the prospective parents selective abortion decision but rather a combination of reasons influenced the outcome of their deliberations. Surely, the parents' background, education, religious convictions and a variety of other factors accounted for their unique assessment of the situation they encountered throughout the process often exceeding any purely objective quantification of the disease. It became most evident that directive counseling in such compounded circumstances has no place in the selective abortion decision (16).

To conclude, we would like to emphasize that although prenatal diagnosis of chromosomal disorders today is a relatively simple and straightforward procedure there are multiple inherent elements and important ramifications which go beyond the technical aspect and these components were highlighted in this paper.

References

1. J.W. Ballantyne. Two lectures on antenatal diagnosis. Brit. Med. J. 1:1525-1529, 1900.

2. T.O. Menees, J.D. Miller and L.E. Holly. Amniography: preliminary report. Amer. J. Roentgen. 24:363-366, 1930.

3. A.W. Liley. The use of amniocentesis and fetal transfusion in erythroblastosis fetalis. Pediatrics. 35: 836-847, 1965.

4. C.J. Epstein and M.S. Golbus. Prenatal diagnosis of genetic diseases. Amer. Scient. 65:703-711, 1977.

5. G. Barsel, S.M. Pueschel, H.A. Hall and D.N. Abuelo. Experience with prenatal diagnosis in Rhode Island. R.I. Med. J. 61:273-278, 1978.

6. NICHD National Registry for Amniocentesis Study Group. Midtrimester amniocentesis for prenatal diagnosis. JAMA. 236:1471-1476, 1976.

7. N.E. Simpson, L. Dallaire, J.R. Miller et al. Prenatal diagnosis of genetic disease in Canada: report of a collaborative study. Can. Med. Assoc. J. 115:739-746, 1976.

8. A. Milunsky. Prenatal diagnosis of genetic disorders. N. Engl. J. Med. 295:377-380, 1976.

9. M. Golbus. The antenatal detection of genetic disorders - current status and future prospects. Obstet. Gynecol. 48:497-506, 1976.

10. A. Milunsky. The Prevention of Genetic Disorders and Mental Retardation. Philadelphia, W.B. Saunders Co., 1975, pp. 238-244.

11. H.L. Nadler. Indications for amniocentesis in the early prenatal detection of genetic disorders. Birth Defects: Orig. Article Series. 8(5):5-9, 1971.

12. B. Santesson, H.O. Akesson, J.A. Book and A. Brosset. Karyotyping human amniotic fluid cells. Lancet 2: 1067, 1969.

13. B. Crandell and T. Lebherz. Prenatal genetic diagnosis

in 350 amniocenteses. <u>Obstet. Gynecol</u>. 48:158-162, 1976.

14. G. Oakley and R.I. Jahiel. Unpublished data. Presented at the Birth Defects Symposium VIII, Albany, New York, November 1977.

15. Z. Stein, M. Susser and A.V. Guterman. Screening programme for prevention of Down's Syndrome. <u>Lancet</u> 1: 305-310, 1973.

16. S.M. Pueschel and E. Clardy. Amniocentesis and selective abortion: factors involved in prospective parents' decision-making. In press.

7

Prenatal Detection
of Neural Tube Defects

Aubrey Milunsky (as summarized by Tamah L. Sadick)

It is a pleasure to share with you some of the more
recent data on prevention of the Neural Tube Defects (NTD's)
through prenatal detection.

The Neural Tube Defects are a consequential spectrum
of major congenital malformations in the sense that one of
these defects is present in every 500 births in the United
States with an incidence twice that in the United Kingdom.
Each year approximately 6,000 to 8,000 infants are born with
these disorders in this country.

The clinical spectrum of these midline deformities of
the central nervous system range from the more severe types
of anencephaly to the enphalocoeles, meningomyelocoeles, and
spina bifidas. Each represents a different expression of
the same basic genetic defect. Associated malformations,
such as anencephaly and a large meningomyelocele, hydrocephalus and spina bifida have been found in the same fetus.
These malformations may also be said to interbreed in the
sense that a patient, for example, may have a child with a
meningomyelocele in one pregnancy and a child with anencephaly in a subsequent pregnancy.

The burden of an NTD depends on the type and extent of
the defect and where it is located. Anencephaly is always
associated with stillbirth or neonatal death. With reference
to the other malformations, the extent of the impairment,
and the degree of physical and mental handicap varies. Of
the approximately half who survive the first 24 hours of

---

*This is a detailed summarization made by Tamah Sadick, Ph.D.,
from the transcribed tape of the speech given by Dr. Aubrey
Milunsky at the symposium "Prevention of Genetic Disease and
Developmental Disabilities," at the 144th Annual Meeting of
the AAAS, February 13, 1978, Washington, D.C.

life, 75% will have severe physical handicap and about 20% moderate to severe mental retardation(1).

The indications for amniocentesis and prenatal studies are best looked at through the family history for the NTD's. There is an increased risk after one child is born with an NTD, and this risk increases with the birth of each affected child. A 3-5% figure for reoccurrence is the one most often given when there has been one previous child affected with an NTD(2,3). However, this figure is adapted from English and United Kingdom studies and may not be applicable to the United States or Canada where the recurrence rate may be more like 1.5 - 1.6%. If one of the parents has been affected with an NTD, the risk of occurrence in a child would be similar to that when there has been a previously affected child(4).

Since Brock and Sutcliff in Edinburgh(5) first described the use of alpha-fetoprotein (AFP) as a diagnostic adjunct for the antenatal detection of the NTD's, this assay has become a major asset. When an open NTD is present, serum or spinal fluid leaks out into the amniotic fluid causing the elevation of the AFP. AFP studies are easily and reliably done in amniotic fluid by electroimmuno diffusion as described by Laurell(6).

Human AFP has been recognized as a fetal-specific alpha-1-globulin since 1956(7). It is normally made by the fetal yolk sac, liver, and G.I. tract(8.9) and may be detectable in fetal blood as early as 29 days in gestation, reaching a peak in fetal blood around 12 weeks of pregnancy and then trailing off to an almost non-detectable level by term(9). You could construct a curve with a peak at about 14 weeks gestation for amniotic fluid alpha-fetoprotein: thus the time to offer these studies in pregnancies at risk for NTD's is about the 14th to 16th week of gestation(5). Normally this protein enters the amniotic fluid in the fetal urine and then spills over into maternal serum(10). In general, adults only make AFP in situations which are unusual, such as in cancer of the liver or in hepatitis.

The curve for this particular protein in maternal serum is very different from that of the amniotic fluid. The peak in maternal serum is between 28-32 weeks in pregnancy, the level rising slowly from about 10-12 weeks and rising steeply through the 15-20 week range. This has important connotations for testing maternal serum.

In situations where there is a defect in the fetus which is open and leaking, and in 90% of the NTD's this is

the case, there is an additional source of egress for the
normal protein into the amniotic fluid. By that token,
other defects that leak in a fetus will be signaled by an
elevation of this particular protein. AFP level elevations
have been found to occur in situations in which there is im-
pending fetal death, various other fetal abnormalities,
twinning, and missed spontaneous abortions, Turner's Syndrome,
congenital nephrosis where the kidney itself is leaking and
there is fetal proteinuria, omphalocele, esophageal atresia,
duodenal atresia, and Meckel's Syndrome(11). Therefore, it
is apparent that the elevated AFP in the amniotic fluid is
non-specific and is not diagnostic of NTD's alone.

In Boston more than 10,000 cases have now been studied
using the amniotic fluid AFP assay(12-14). The samples have
come from various laboratories and hospitals in the United
States. Of these 10,000, 1,525 had previously delivered a
child with an NTD. Twenty-four of those whose outcomes
were tabulated which was less than the 1,525 were found to
be carrying another fetus with an NTD. This is 3% of our
sample on those whose pregnancy outcome we know. We, however, estimate that the figure should be more like 1.6% because we have not heard of any deliveries in which a child
was born with an NTD which we did not diagnose earlier. To
our knowledge, we have not missed any open neural tube defect, and we have diagnosed some 95.

Thus, the recurrence figure for the United States may
in effect be more like 1.6% as we have already mentioned.

Samples obtained for routine cytogenetic studies because of advanced maternal age primarily to exclude chromosomal disorders were also subjected to AFP assay. We found
20 or 1 in 400-417 (0.25%) which turned out to have some
kind of open and leaking NTD. Every amniotic fluid sample
obtained for antenatal genetic studies should be examined
routinely for AFP as well(15). This draws attention perhaps to the maternal age relationship for neural tube defects which has been published but has not been carefully
studied as yet.

The experience with NTD's (Fig. 1)(15) illustrates that
there is a wide variation (2.25 - 44 mg.%) of AFP concentration in such defects. The highest values were found among
the anencephaly cases. Note the steep decline in concentration with advancing gestation even in the presence of an
open neural tube defect. The shaded area represents +3 SD.
above the mean based on 900 cases of known normal outcome.
Using 4 or 5 SD. above mean values gives even better dis-

crimination between true positives and lesser elevations of
AFP associated with normal pregnancies(14).

False negative results of AFP assay are largely confined almost exclusively to closed neural tube defects.

There are, however, two other major reasons for false

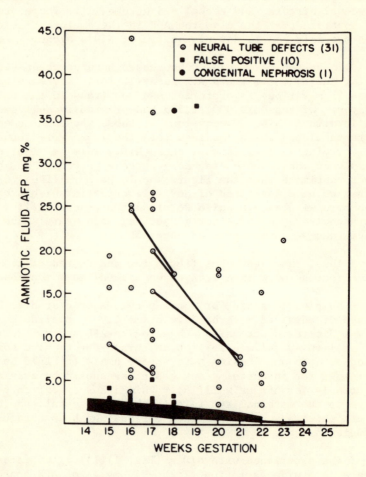

Fig. 1. AFP concentrations in neural tube defects, in "normal
progeny with elevated values (false positives), and in 1 case
of congenital nephrosis. Note the steep decline in concentration with advancing gestation even in the presence of an open
neural tube defect. The shaded area represents the mean +3
S.D. based on assays of about 900 cases of known normal outcome.

negatives(13,14). Should the amniocentesis be performed at
a point in gestation at which the AFP has already declined,
a false negative result might be obtained. To illustrate
this, a pediatrician herself was found to be carrying an
anencephalic fetus on AFP assay at 16 weeks of pregnancy.
She, however, waited 5 weeks before she elected to terminate
the pregnancy. By that time, there was an appreciable drop
in the AFP. If one then should neglect to do an amniocentesis for AFP assay before 21 or 22 weeks of pregnancy, the
elevation will probably be missed (Fig. 1)(15).

In the published literature it may be noted that there
is an almost 100% detection rate in cases involving anencephaly diagnosed before 24 weeks of pregnancy. In one case,
however, to the doctor's chagrin, he had tapped the patient's
bladder rather than the amniotic sac and sent urine instead
of amniotic fluid to the laboratory. A false negative result was obtained, and the case was missed. An identical
situation obtained in a woman carrying a fetus with spina
bifida.

We estimate that urine may be obtained in 1 of every
300-500 cases. Aspiration of urine instead of amniotic
fluid is another reason for false negative results. Because
of this, we now recommend that all fluids sent for AFP assay
by assessed for odor, ph, protein concentration, and amount
and type of cellular material(12,13,14).

The major problem facing us today is when an elevated
value is found in the presence of an apparently normal fetus
or subsequently delivered newborn(12-14). In our lab, generally, we are finding about 1/1,000 cases with false positive values, a false positive rate of 0.1%.

Of the 10,000 cases we have studied, pregnancy outcome
is known in about 5,000.

In 66 of these cases, approximately 9.7% of cases,
elevated AFP was found because fetal blood contaminated the
sample. It is known that the level of AFP in fetal blood
is about 150-200 times higher than it is in amniotic fluid.
Just a couple of drops of fetal blood in the amniotic fluid
may lead to significant elevation of the AFP concentration.
It has been calculated that as little as $50\mu l$. of fetal
blood in a 10 ml. amniotic fluid sample may as much as
double the AFP concentration. We now routinely assay by the
Betke Kleihauer test(16) for fetal hemoglobin in all samples
where an elevated (more than +3 SD.) AFP concentration is
determined. In this respect, however, when samples come
from other laboratories, the amniotic fluid usually has been

centrifuged immediately or soon after aspiration and the red
blood cells thrown to the bottom leaving only the supinate
to be sent for the assay. In these cases if an elevated
AFP just above +3 SD. is found, we don't know if there was
fetal blood contaminating the sample if there are no cells
around to test.

The recommended procedure for prenatal diagnosis of
open NTD's is to perform an amniocentesis between 14 and
16 weeks' gestation, reserving 1-2ml. of whole (unspun)
amniotic fluid. A few microliters of the sample are used
for the AFP assay with the remainder available for fetal
blood testing. If the AFP level is elevated, the remaining
whole fluid is centrifuged, the supinate tested for fetal
hemoglobin, and the pellet tested for fetal erythrocytes
(14). We also recommend that one never take an action on
a single reading or single assay. After all, it could have
been someone else's fluid that was assayed, which has hap-
pened. A group of about 50 amniotic fluids was sent to us
from a distant laboratory, and after assaying all those
samples, we reported that a particular case had a very high
level of AFP. Action was taken and the pregnancy terminated
A normal fetus was found.

Five months later, a child with anencephaly was delivered to the patient listed immediately below that patient.
The technician in the other laboratory had confused the
tube numbers, and we later confirmed that because we had
all the fluids and retested them.

In some cases we have no explanation at all for false
positives. One of our patients has done it again, in the
sense that another elevated alpha-fetoprotein was found.
In this case, however, there was suspicion of nephrosis.

Another problem complicating interpretation of AFP
results is in the determination of the gestational age of
the fetus. Since the AFP value varies with gestational age,
the cut-off point is different for each week of gestation.
Because of this, ultrasound prior to amniocentesis for assessment of fetal age is strongly recommended. The matter
becomes consequential, of course, only when a marginal AFP
above +3 SD. is determined.

A difference in 3 weeks may on occasion make the differ
ence between the decision to terminate a pregnancy or to con
tinue. In addition, there is a need to educate the obstetrician about the importance of the 14-16 week time indication for study since accurate conclusions from the AFP assay
may become more difficult toward the end of the second tri-

mester. If necessary, in cases of a marginal elevation of
the AFP value, a repeat amniocentesis can be done. However,
it is important to note that a normal AFP value at a later
gestational age may not invalidate an earlier positive result and ultrasound and amniography are excellent adjunctive
techniques to identify anencephaly, hydrocephalus, and spina
bifida.

In our hands, this procedure has led to a false positive
error rate of only 0.1% allowing for confident recommendation
of this assay for all patients undergoing amniocentesis at
the appropriate stage of pregnancy.

The most important consideration and perhaps reservation
which attend the use of the alpha-fetoprotein assay in amniotic fluid is the need to know the normal range at the
proper gestational age in every laboratory that provides
these kinds of studies. Almost once a month our laboratory
receives a call from a doctor who will say he has a value of
such and such deciliters and wants to know what it means.
When told to ask the laboratory that performed the study
whether it is normal or not, the answer is usually that
he/she has asked but was told that the laboratory is in the
business of measuring substances and not practicing medicine.
This is a brand of charlatanism. It is obvious that there
is a need for a laboratory to establish its norms and not to
essentially hide behind the question in the sense in which
they put it, "When we do a blood count, we do not tell you
whether or not the patient is anemic, we just tell you the
hemoglobin is such and such".

It is important to know that 9 out of 10 babies with
neural tube closure defects are born to women who have never
previously had an affected child. Thus prenatal studies
are sampling only 10% of the possible cases. Thus, the
developing rationale has been to look at maternal serum on
all pregnancies to identify the other 90% of cases that do
occur.

In the United Kingdom (UK), maternal serum AFP screening has proved to be a potentially valuable non-invasive
tool for the early detection in utero of these remaining
90% of NTD's and is now becoming part of routine obstetrical
care.

The findings from the screenings of 18,985 pregnancies
in the U.K. Collaborative Study(17) drew attention to the
ability by radioimmunoassay of AFP in maternal serum to
detect at 16 to 18 weeks of pregnancy in a prospective way,
88% of anencephalic pregnancies and 79% of those pregnancies

with spina bifida. However, in 3% of normal singleton pregnancies positive results were also found, a false positive
rate or noise in the serum of about 3%.

In the anencephalic and those pregnancies with spina
bifida, AFP levels exceeded by 2.5 times the normal median
value.

When a test was found to be positive, the sequence pursued was, and is, as follows: sonography to check out dates
because of the climbing levels of concentration of AFP from
15 weeks to 32 weeks of gestation and to rule out multiple
pregnancies which also often raise the AFP levels, and then,
of course, if everything checks out, an amniocentesis to
identify an abnormal fetus.

We have now studied 3,000 cases in Boston and have
really duplicated the United Kingdom results. Our false
positive rate is smaller but because our figures are small,
we are unable to make a final statement on this. It may
reflect a single rather than a pooled laboratory experience.

There is now considerable discussion about developing
a national strategy to provide routine screening of all
pregnancies in the United States. Certain limiations and
reservations are apparent even before the pilot studies have
been completed(1,18,19).

Radioimmunoassay of maternal serum AFP concentration is
optimally done at 16 to 18 weeks of gestation. The normal
AFP concentration is different for each gestational week,
and normal levels must be established by each laboratory.
Maternal blood drawn before 15 weeks yields much lower "detection" rate and after 18 weeks of gestation, time constraints are extremely tight if the parents elect termination
of the pregnancy. The time of maternal serum study is,
therefore, crucial and may be compounded by the substantial
number, 20 to 40% of (especially urban) women who attend
for their first prenatal visit after 18 weeks' gestation.

The need to know the exact gestational age is hindered
by the frequently incorrect estimated dates by the patient
and common inaccuracies of clinical examination.

If the measurement is made at what is thought to be 15
weeks of pregnancy but is in effect really 20 weeks, there
is going to be a very great difference not only in the level
but in the interpretation. The value at 20 weeks, if the
pregnancy is truly 20 weeks, will be fine; but if the value
is that same level and the pregnancy is only 15 weeks, that

is a gross abnormality. Thus, ultrasound scanning to assess
fetal age accurately is a key ancillary service for the development of an AFP screening program but such service is
at present not always available or not of sufficiently high
enough quality in many areas of the United States.

The assay itself for AFP in maternal serum provides the
least problem. The radioimmunoassays are accurate, repro-
ducibility is excellent, the assay is reasonably inexpensive
and can be automated. What is problematical, of course, is
that in the United States the FDA has yet to license the use
of the antiserum for the alpha-fetoprotein. Therefore, it
is still illegal to have studies done across state lines on
a fee-by-service basis.

Still not clear is the frequency of an elevated maternal
serum with a normal amniotic fluid AFP or the frequency of
an elevated amniotic fluid AFP where the maternal AFP level
has been normal and yet there is an NTD in the fetus.

We are also finding racial differences between results
on blacks and whites and would have offered unnecessary amniocenteses to a number of blacks. Perhaps the black women
are less likely to know their dates or pregnancy stage than
the white patients, but we really do not know why these
racial differences exist.

Certain prerequisites are required if a national strategy for maternal serum screening is to develop. Any public
health plan offering such a service would need to emphasize
equal access, voluntarism, and informed consent.

Both the professional and the public need to understand
the screening rather than the diagnostic nature of this tool.
They should appreciate that an elevated serum AFP may mean,
in addition to NTD's, multiple pregnancy, certain obstetric
complications (threatened abortion, fetal death or Rh disease, other congenital malformations), maternal disease
(e.g. viral hepatitis) or may signal the birth of babies
with low birth weights.

It may be that detection of elevated values--those
2 1/2 times above the median would be very valuable in
selecting out high-risk pregnancies, especially those end-
ing in low birth weight babies, in prematurity, postmaturity,
stillbirths, or other difficulties in pregnancy(20,21).

Such information alerting the obstetrician to high-risk
pregnancies ultimately might provide benefits far in excess
of that obtained from screening only for NTD's. These would

include decreasing the frequency of prematurity, low birth
weight babies, and thus increased incidence of cerebral pal-
sy, mental retardation (I.Q. < 50) and other neurological
deficiencies(20,21).

Screening centers would not only have to provide reliable assay for serum AFP but the ancillary services as well.
The availability of dependable obstetric ultrasound services
in close association with a laboratory experienced in amniotic fluid AFP assays and cell culture are a necessity,
since fetal karyotyping is often requested once amniotic
fluid is obtained. The availability of a good genetic counseling service would also be a prerequisite.

The cost vs. benefit equation invariably intrudes upon
any major plan for preventive medicine. Although the serum
assay would probably cost less than $1 per case for screen-
ing, only limited cost estimates are available in the United
States for care of the patients with NTD's(22). Very rough
calculations based on some as yet unproved assumptions, with
exclusion of potential income loss by patient and parent,
suggest that the cost to society of care would be more than
10 times the cost of an effective screening program. Over
40 years, ignoring inflation, the cost of care might well
exceed a total of $1 billion. These cost estimates depend
on a high degree of patient compliance, as assessed in the
United Kingdom calculations(23). Although the vast majority
of the American public is not opposed to elective abortion
of a seriously defective fetus, considerable numbers of
pregnant women may elect not to have serum AFP screening
because of their antipathy to abortion.

When this is coupled with the large number of women who
come after the 18th week of pregnancy for the first prenatal
visit, which is too late, it becomes obvious that many potentially detectable NTD's will be missed. Costs then might
outweigh the benefits.

Though we are not as yet ready for institution of
maternal serum AFP screening on a national basis, we are
confident that maternal serum AFP screening, after FDA
licensing of reagents, will eventually become part of routine obstetric practice in the United States. We believe
that the optimal approach is the development of regional
centers with all the required ancillary services. In this
way, both patient and physician would be assured of the
best possible care with the greatest possible cost efficiency.

References

1. A. Milunsky, Maternal serum AFP screening, N. Engl. J. Med. 298(13):738-739, 1978.

2. C. O. Carter and J. A. F. Roberts, The risk of recurrence after two children with central nervous system malformations, Lancet I:306-308, 1967.

3. C. O. Carter, Genetics of common malformations. Recent Advances in Pediatrics, Fourth edition. Edited by D. Gardner, D. Hull. London. J&A Churchill, Ltd., 1971.

4. B. Field and C. Kerr, Offspring of parents with spina bifida occulta, Lancet II:1257, 1975.

5. D. J. H. Brock and R. G. Sutcliffe, Alpha-fetoprotein in the antenatal diagnosis of anencephaly and spina bifida, Lancet, July 29, 1972, 197-199.

6. C. B. Laurell, Quantitative estimation of proteins by electrophoresis in agarose gel containing antibodies, Annl. Biochem. 15:45-52, 1966.

7. C. G. Bergstrand and B. Czar, Demonstration of a new protein fraction in serum from the human fetus, Scand. J. Clin. Lab. Invest. 8:174, 1956.

8. D. Getlin and M. Balsman, Serum alpha-fetoprotein, albumin and gamma G-globulin in the human conceptus, J. Clin. Invest. 45:1826, 1966.

9. D. Getlin, A. Perricelli, and G. M. Getlin, Synthesis of alpha-fetoprotein by liver, yolk sac, and gastrointestinal tract of the human conceptus. Cancer Res. 32:979, 1972.

10. M. Seppala and E. Rusolaliti, Alpha-fetoprotein in amniotic fluid: An index of gestational age. Am. J. Obst. Gynecol. 114:595, 1972.

11. A. Milunsky, Ed., The Prevention of Genetic Disease and Mental Retardation, Philadelphia, W. B. Saunders Co., 1975.

12. A. Milunsky and E. Alpert, Prenatal diagnosis of neural tube defects I. Problems and pitfalls: Analysis of 2495 cases using the alpha-fetoprotein assay. Obst. Gynecol. 48:6-12, 1976.

13.   A. Milunsky and E. Alpert, Prenatal diagnosis of neural
      tube defects. II. Analysis of false positive and false
      negative alpha-fetoprotein results. Obst. Gynecol.48:
      1-5, 1976.

14.   Margaret E. Kimball, A. Milunsky, and E. Alpert, Pre-
      natal diagnosis of neural tube defects III. A reevalu-
      ation of the alpha-fetoprotein assay. Obst. Gynecol.
      49:532-536, 1977.

15.   A. Milunsky, Amniotic fluid alpha-fetoprotein assay
      for neural tube defects: Practice, problems, and pit-
      falls, Excerpta Medica International Congress Series
      No. 411, Human Genetics, Proceedings of Fifth Inter-
      national Congress on Human Genetics. Mexico City 10-15
      Oct., 1976. Excerpta Medica Amsterdanm ISBN 90 219
      03377.

16.   D. Kleihauer, H. Braun, and K. Betke, Wemonstraton von
      fetalen halmoglobin in die erythrozyten eines
      Blutausstriches, Klin. Wochenstr. 35:637-638, 1957.

17.   U.K. Collaborative Study on Alpha-fetoprotein in rela-
      tion to neural tube defects. Maternal serum - alpha-
      fetoprotein measurement in antenatal screening for
      anencephaly and spina bifida in early pregnancy, Lancet
      I:1323-1332, 1977.

18.   J. N. Macri, and R. R. Weiss, Birth defects original
      art ser. 13, 3D, 191, 1977. J. Am. Med. Soc. 238:
      141, 1977.

19.   William Check, Mass screening for open spina bifida
      needs careful consideration, Med. News JAMA 238:1441,
      1977.

20.   D. J. H. Brock, L. Barron, P. Jelen, M. Watt, J. B.
      Scringeour. Maternal serum alpha-fetoprotein measure-
      ments as an early indication for birth weight. Lancet
      II:267-268, 1977.

21.   N. Wald, H. Cuckle, G. M. Sterrat, J. Bennett, A. C.
      Turnbull, Maternal serum alpha-fetoprotein and low
      birth weight, Lancet II:268-270, 1977.

22.   D. B. Shurtleff, P. W. Hayden, J. D. Loeser, et. al.,
      Myelodysplasia: decision for death or diability. N.
      Engl. J. Med. 291:1005-1011, 1974.

23. S. P. Hagard, P. Carter, and R. G. Milne, Screening for spina bifida cystica: A cost-benefit analysis, Brit. J. Prev. Soc. Med. 30:40-53, 1976.

Prenatal Diagnosis by Fetoscopy and Fetal Blood Sampling Including Initial Attempts to Diagnose Duchenne Muscular Dystrophy

8

Maurice J. Mahoney and John C. Hobbins

Amniocentesis has been the primary technic of diagnosis in this beginning era of fetal medicine. We have seen increasingly sophisticated biochemical and genetic methods applied to amniotic fluid and amniotic fluid cells. A large number of diagnoses have been made possible with these methods but many others have not. Today other technics are being developed to augment amniocentesis. These have evolved to overcome the limited view of fetal physiology and anatomy which are provided by study of amniotic fluid and cells. Two of the new applications have already demonstrated exciting potential for a much expanded diagnostic and therapeutic approach to the human fetus. One is ultrasonography whose sophistication now provides detailed representations of both surface and internal organ anatomy (1). Real time ultrasound gives a dynamic view of the fetal heart or the entire fetus moving in utero. The second advance has been the development of fetoscopy and fetal biopsy. With these technics parts of the fetus can be visualized directly using light brought into the uterus; in addition, the fetal blood stream can be sampled or a small fragment of skin can be biopsied. This chapter will outline the technics of fetoscopy and fetal blood sampling, their potential uses for prenatal diagnosis, and the initial attempts toward finding a method of diagnosis for Duchenne muscular dystrophy. Other reviews of the history and method of fetoscopy and of the diagnostic potential of fetal blood are listed for further reference (2).

Fetoscopy

After several years of using larger endoscopes with attendant high risks to the pregnancy, perinatologists have

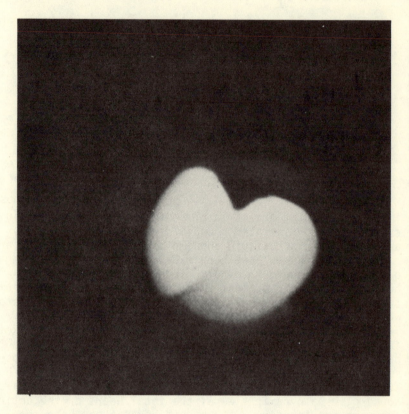

Figure 1. Two fetal toes at 18 weeks (menstrual) gestation, as seen through the fetoscope. Magnification about 20 X.

turned to a small diameter fetoscope which can be inserted
into the uterus through the abdominal wall with minimal
trauma. A major problem of a small instrument, though, is a
limited field of view. The instrument has a diameter of
2.0 mm or less and, when inserted into the amniotic cavity,
is housed in a cannula of 2.0 - 3.0 mm. The cannula is large
enough to allow passage of a blood sampling needle or biopsy
forceps alongside the lens. Light is taken into the uterus
on fibers and the image is returned either by a fiberoptic
lens or a solid self-focusing lens. The angle of visualization is about 70^0 and objects are in focus through a depth
of 2 cm. These parameters permit 2 - 4 sq cm of surface
area to be in view at one time. For a pregnancy at 18 weeks
gestation, this viewing area shows only part of a fetal hand
or foot without moving the fetoscope. Figure 1 is a photo-
graph through a fetoscope showing the ventral surface of two
fetal toes at 18 menstrual weeks.

Prior to insertion of the fetoscope, careful ultrasound
information is obtained using either grey scale or real time
sonography. This information enables the fetoscopist to
select an entry site which will be as safe as possible for
the fetus and which will place the desired parts of the fetus
or placenta into view. Real time ultrasound is also used
during the procedure to help locate specific fetal parts.
Local anesthesia is injected at the entry site on the
mother's abdomen and is usually the only drug given during
the procedure. If fetal sedation is desired, diazepam or
meperidine can also be given to the mother.

Visualization of the fetus is optimum between 15 and
18 weeks gestation. At this stage the fetus is relatively
small compared to the surrounding amniotic fluid volume and
the fluid is very clear. We and others have been able to
identify and study specific parts of the fetus and several
fetal behaviors (3). Localized areas have included close
views of digits, joints, external genitalia, and umbilical
cord. Details of the skin surface including hair, nails,
and pores can be appreciated. At the head and face one can
see ears, closed eyes with fused eyelids, the nose and mouth,
and even the palate, but the parts can only be seen singly
and a panoramic view of the face is not possible. Fetal
movements such as thumb sucking, swallowing, grasping, and
defecation have been observed through the fetoscope in the
16 to 18 week fetus.

We rarely attempt total visualization of the fetus but
instead focus on parts of the fetus which may yield diagnostic information regarding a specific anatomic defect. With
this limited purpose, fetoscopy can successfully examine the
fetus about 90% of the time.

Diagnosis by fetoscopy

Several pregnancies have been examined which were at
risk for limb abnormalities or neural tube defects (3-5).
The indications for examination are listed in the table.

Limbs or digits examined because of risk for:
    Arthrogryposis multiplex congenita
    Laurence-Moon-Biedl-Bardot syndrome
    Absent limb
    Meckel syndrome
    Holt-Oram syndrome
    Split hand syndrome
    Ellis-van Creveld syndrome
    Polydactyly (with other major defects)

Trunk examined because of risk for:
    Spina bifida
    Exomphalos

In the majority of these examinations normal fetal parts
have been seen and normal infants were born at the end of
gestation. The first positive diagnosis using fetoscopy was
in a pregnancy at risk for the Ellis-van Creveld syndrome (5)
This autosomal recessive disorder consists of dwarfism,
congenital heart disease, and polydactyly. The presence of
an extra digit established the diagnosis.
    Spina bifida defects have been visualized in pregnancies
at very high risk for this lesion because of an elevated
alpha-fetoprotein concentration in amniotic fluid. In a
very instructive and satisfying case, Rodeck and Campbell
reported examining the back of a fetus and finding no
abnormality in a pregnancy in which spina bifida was suspect
from ultrasound and alpha-fetoprotein data (4). A normal
infant with no sign of a neural tube defect was born.
    Fetoscopy with currently available instruments has
definite limitations. Severe abnormalities of surface
anatomy can be recognized, but small variations from normal
cannot. If one of the components of a birth defect syndrome
is an extra or missing digit, a major cleft, or some other
gross abnormality, fetoscopy can be useful for diagnosis.
On the other hand, if the dysmorphology consists of an unusual shape of the eyes, moderately shortened limbs, or asym-
metry of the skull, fetoscopy would not help. Also, fetoscopy is an invasive technic and carries risk for the fetus
and for the pregnancy. In the future, ultrasonography will
probably become sufficiently sophisticated to define aspects
of surface anatomy that can only be seen by fetoscopy today.

Fetal Blood Sampling

Of perhaps more interest than the fetus itself for the fetal diagnostician is the placenta with its circulation of fetal blood. Small veins and arteries, which branch from the umbilical vessels, course along the chorionic plate at the inside surface of the placenta. These vessels with connecting capillaries form a closed circulation of fetal blood.

In the placental substance, surrounding the fetal capillaries, are pools of maternal blood. It is from the fetal circulation in the placenta that successful attempts at sampling fetal blood have been made rather than from the body of the fetus.

Two methods for obtaining fetal blood have been developed. One utilizes fetoscopy (6) and the other consists of ultrasonically directed placental aspiration (7).

Fetoscopy affords direct visualization of the fetal vessels on the chorionic plate and vessel puncture can be accomplished in a controlled manner. A 25 - 27 gauge sampling needle is inserted into the cannula alongside the lens of the fetoscope. When a vessel is located the sampling needle is advanced to puncture it under direct vision. A diagram of this method is shown in figure 2. Most often, blood cannot be aspirated directly from the lumen of the vessel because of the small bore and long length of the sampling needle. Instead, the needle is withdrawn from the vessel and blood is aspirated with a syringe as it spurts into the surrounding amniotic fluid. Samples of 0.05 - 0.15 ml are collected and bleeding stops after several seconds. The syringe and sampling needle must contain anticoagulant. We have used both heparin and citrate successfully.

Blood sampling via fetoscopy is somewhat more difficult when the placenta is anterior but can be satisfactorily accomplished with experience. The samples obtained by an experienced operator using this method are often uncontaminated by maternal blood and only rarely contain 50% or more maternal blood. If the gestational age of the fetus is 18 - 19 weeks, the most common time for attempting fetoscopic sampling, fetal blood volume depletion is expected to be less than 3% (8).

Placental aspiration is performed with a 19 - 21 gauge spinal needle. The position of the placenta and the depth of the chorionic plate are estimated from the sonogram and the needle is advanced to the interface of the chorionic plate in the amniotic cavity. Blood is then aspirated and immediately checked by a Coulter electronic cell sizer for the presence of fetal cells. Fetal red blood cells have a mean cell volume about one and one-half times larger than adult red cells at midgestation. The cell sizer will detect

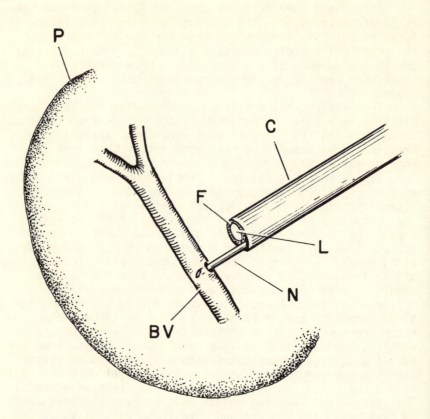

Figure 2. Diagram of the distal end of a fetoscope with a blood sampling needle in a placental blood vessel.
P = placenta; BV = blood vessel; F = fiberoptics for light; L = lens; C = cannula; N = needle.

a 5% contamination of fetal blood by maternal blood or
maternal blood by fetal blood. If a satisfactory sample
was not obtained, the needle is redirected and another sample
is aspirated. Contamination with maternal blood, often in
large amounts, is common with this method, although pure
samples of fetal blood occasionally result.
    A satisfactory blood sample for fetal diagnosis of the
hemoglobinopathies, the most common diagnosis sought to date,
will be obtained on first attempt about 90% of the time.
A second attempt will succeed in most of the initial failures
so that diagnostic information is usually available to the
requesting family. A good plasma sample is more difficult
to obtain than a good red cell sample because of dilution
with amniotic fluid. Experience with obtaining plasma
is still small, but presumably the failure rate will be
higher.

Diagnosis by fetal blood sampling

    The first attempts at fetal diagnosis using fetal blood
were for the major hemoglobinopathies, sickle cell disease
and beta-thalassemia. Diagnosis depended upon the in vitro
synthesis of hemoglobins by the aspirated fetal red blood
cells. Details of these investigations are the subject of
another chapter.
    After the initial successes using fetal red cells, we
began attempts to use white blood cells and plasma for diagnoses. At this time, diagnosis of chronic granulomatous
disease has been made from absence of nitroblue tetrazolium
reduction by fetal polymorphonuclear leukocytes (9), and
diagnosis of classic hemophilia has been accomplished by
finding deficiency of factor VIII coagulant antigen in fetal
plasma (10). Both of these diseases are X-linked disorders
and the male fetuses were at 50% risk.
    The diseases noted above, plus most other hemoglobino-
pathies, clotting disorders, and white cell disorders,
cannot be diagnosed today using amniotic fluid or cells
found in the fluid. A small sample of fetal blood is
necessary. This is also true of many other inherited and
acquired fetal diseases. Some disorders for which diagnosis
with fetal blood may be possible are listed in the following
table.

    Diagnosis using red cell enzymes:

        Pyruvate kinase deficiency
        Argininemia

Diagnosis using white blood cells:

Agranulocytosis
Agammaglobulinemia (B cells)
Combined immunodeficiency disease (T and B cells)
Chediak-Higashi syndrome

Diagnosis using platelets:

Wiskott-Aldrich syndrome

Diagnosis using plasma:

Deficiency of major plasma proteins
Urea cycle metabolic errors

In addition to the wide range of diagnostic possibilities,
fetal blood sampling also offers the hope of developing
monitored therapy for specific fetal diseases. Drug
therapy or genetic engineering (replacement by a normal gene
or gene product) will probably require access to the fetal
blood stream and may require multiple samples of blood over
a period of time. Devising safe methods to accomplish
these goals is an exciting challenge for fetal medicine
and fetal research and one which seems possible of success
in light of recent advances.

Fetal Skin Biopsy

Fetal blood is not the only tissue which is easily
accessible with fetoscopy. Small 1 mm skin biopsies can
easily be obtained from the scalp or from the trunk. The
tissue fragment can be analyzed anatomically or biochemicall
or can be put in tissue culture to obtain a quickly growing
cell culture.
We have biopsied fetal skin in one diagnostic situation
a pregnancy at risk for the harlequin type of congenital
ichthyosis. Normal skin was obtained and a normal child has
been born. Future uses of skin biopsy may include measurement of tissue drug levels, assessment of nutritional status
or a search for teratogenic chemicals.

Risks of Fetoscopy and Fetal Blood Sampling

Direct visualization of the fetus and aspiration of
fetal blood require invasive procedures, significantly more
invasive than amniocentesis and ultrasonography. World
experience is small at this time but some estimates of risk
can be made. Acute fetal deaths have occurred from both
fetoscopy and placental aspiration; these have resulted

because of amnionitis, miscarriage, placental abruption, and
fetal exsanguination. Exsanguination has only been a complication of the placental aspiration technic. Thus far, significant maternal morbidity has not been reported.

The largest fetoscopy series, our own at Yale-New Haven
Medical Center, has a 3% fetal mortality (2 deaths) in 65
continuing pregnancies. The largest placental aspiration
series, 96 pregnancies at University College Hospital in
London, has a 10% fetal loss in the total series and a 3%
loss in the last third of the series (11). Our own combined
series of fetoscopy and placental aspiration in 63 completed
pregnancies shows 9% premature deliveries. This is one and
one-half times the prematurity rate in a control population
and suggests a higher risk of prematurity after these procedures. We also know that fetal blood is transferred to
the maternal circulation during fetoscopy or aspiration, and
we believe that anti-Rh(D) globulin is indicated for Rh negative mothers unless the fetus can be clearly shown to be
Rh negative also using fetal blood cells.

Further delineation of risks for the fetus or mother,
and measures to minimize those risks, are extremely important aspects in the continued development of fetal medicine.

Duchenne Muscular Dystrophy

Duchenne muscular dystrophy (DMD) is the most common
and severe muscular dystrophy of childhood. It is an
X-linked trait and thus disease is seen almost exclusively
in boys. Onset of disease symptoms occurs before age five
and death in the late teens or twenties. The molecular or
biochemical cause of the disease is as yet unknown, but the
progressive muscular wasting is accompanied by markedly
elevated activities of muscle enzymes in the circulation.
Creatine phosphokinase (CPK) activity is especially elevated
and this elevation is highest in early infancy before symptoms
are recognized. It is now appreciated that increased CPK
activity is present in the newborn period in some, and
perhaps all, boys with DMD (12).

Measurement of CPK activity in amniotic fluid has not
proved useful for prenatal diagnosis of DMD, nor has any
other parameter. Without a method for specific diagnosis,
many women, who are either proven carriers of the DMD gene
or possible carriers by virtue of an affected relative, choose
not to have children or to have only girls. If a decision
to have only girls is made, the prospective mother would
have the sex of her fetus determined by amniocentesis and
terminate any pregnancy with a male fetus.

To address the need for a specific method of prenatal
diagnosis, we have measured CPK activity in fetal plasma
of several control fetuses and several male fetuses at risk

for DMD. Plasma was obtained via fetoscopy or placental
aspiration at 19 - 21 weeks gestation. We undertook these
measurements with the hypothesis that if the genetic defect
in DMD led to extremely elevated plasma CPK activities in
newborns, a similar elevation might well be present in the
fetus by 18 gestational weeks.

Data from 30 control fetuses showed a range of CPK
activity of 0 - 120 IU/l (adult normal range 0 - 85 IU/l).
Plasma from one at risk fetus had an activity of 540 IU/l.
This pregnancy was terminated and fetal muscle pathology
was strongly suggestive of a progressive muscular dystrophy
(13). Since that time we have examined several more at risk
pregnancies. In one of these pregnancies, measurement of
a normal fetal CPK activity at 21 weeks gestation (60 IU/l)
was followed by birth of a boy with DMD (14). Umbilical
cord blood had a CPK activity of 3300 IU/l and serum at 4 mo
of age measured 14,700 IU/l. This experience clearly states
that CPK activity measurements will not be satisfactory for
the prenatal diagnosis of DMD.

An explanation for our experience with CPK activity and
fetal DMD is being sought. The disease is probably hetero-
geneous in different families; if so, CPK elevation may occur
early in fetal life in some and late in others. Women who
are carriers of DMD and have an elevated CPK activity when
not pregnant usually have a normal CPK activity during pregnancy. This poorly understood phenomenon may influence
fetal CPK also and do so to a greater extent in some pregnancies than in others. Finally, the association of an
elevated CPK and dystrophic muscle in the first diagnosed
case may have been fortuitous and unrelated.

An alternative to the measurement of plasma enzyme
activities for the prenatal diagnosis of DMD may lie in
investigations of fetal red blood cells. Several difference
between red blood cells from normal boys and from boys with
DMD have been noted (15). Unfortunately, the differences
between DMD cells and normal cells have not been large and
the findings have been difficult to reproduce in different
laboratories. Nonetheless, pursuit of a reproducible red
cell difference that may be reflected in fetal cells seems
warranted in our search for a reliable method of prenatal
diagnosis.

Summary

Amniocentesis provided an initial diagnostic approach
the human fetus. This approach is now being followed by
newer technics in an attempt to obtain more diagnostic info
mation and to develop therapies. Fetoscopy will provide
visual anatomic information about the fetus at midpregnancy
and has become a valuable method for obtaining a sample of

fetal blood or a small skin biopsy.
  The availability of fetal blood has made possible diagnoses of hemoglobin, white blood cell, and clotting disorders
in the fetus which heretofore could not be accomplished.
Initial hopes that Duchenne muscular dystrophy could be
diagnosed by measuring fetal plasma CPK activity have not
been confirmed, however, and other approaches to the diagnosis of Duchenne dystrophy, perhaps with red blood cells,
must by pursued.

References

1. J. C. Hobbins and F. Winsberg. Ultrasonography in
   Obstetrics and Gynecology (Williams & Wilkins, Baltimore,
   1977); R. C. Sanders and A. E. James, Jr., Ultrasonography in Obstetrics and Gynecology (Appleton-Century-
   Crofts, New York, 1977).
2. B. P. Alter and D. G. Nathan, Clinics in Haematology 7,
   195 (1978); J. C. Hobbins and M. J. Mahoney, Clin. Obstet.
   Gynecol. 19, 341 (1976).
3. R. J. Benzie, in Embryology and Pathogenesis and Prenatal
   Diagnosis, D. Bergsma and R. B. Lowry, Eds. Birth Defects
   Original Article Series 13(3D), 181 (1977).
4. J. B. Scrimgeour, in Antenatal Diagnosis of Genetic
   Disease, A. E. H. Emery, Ed. (Churchill Livingstone,
   Edinburgh, 1973) pp. 49-52; K. M. Laurence, J. F. Pearson,
   R. Prosser, C. Richards, I. Rocker, Lancet 1, 1120 (1974);
   I. Rocker, K. M. Laurence, Lancet 1, 716 (1978);
   C. H. Rodeck and S. Campbell, Lancet 1, 1128 (1978).
5. M. J. Mahoney and J. C. Hobbins, New Engl. J. Med. 297,
   258 (1977).
6. J. C. Hobbins and M. J. Mahoney, New Engl. J. Med. 290,
   1065 (1974); J. E. Patrick, T. B. Perry, R. A. H. Kinch,
   Am. J. Obstet. Gynecol. 119, 539 (1974).
7. Y. W. Kan, C. Valenti, R. Guidotti, V. Carnazza, R. F.
   Rieder, Lancet 1, 79 (1974).
8. J. C. Hobbins and M. J. Mahoney, Lancet 2, 107 (1975).
9. P. E. Newburger, H. J. Cohen, S. B. Rothchild, J. C.
   Hobbins, S. E. Malawista, M. J. Mahoney, submitted for
   publication.
10. M. J. Mahoney, L. Hoyer, S. Firschein, J. Lazarchick,
    B. Forget, J. Hobbins, Am. J. Human Genetics (abstract),
    in press.
11. C. B. Modell and D. Fairweather, personal communication.
12. D. Gardner-Medwin, Arch. Dis. Childh. 51, 982 (1976).
13. M. J. Mahoney, F. P. Haseltine, J. C. Hobbins, B. Q.
    Banker, C. T. Caskey, M. S. Golbus, New Engl. J. Med.
    297, 968 (1977).

14. M. S. Golbus, J. D. Stephens, J. C. Hobbins, F. P.
Haseltine, C. T. Caskey, B. Q. Banker, M. J. Mahoney,
submitted for publication.
15. J. L. Howland, <u>Nature</u> 251, 724 (1974); D. W. Matheson an
J. L. Howland, <u>Science</u> 184, 165 (1974); A. D. Roses,
M. H. Herbstreith, S. H. Appel, <u>Nature</u> 254, 350 (1975);
R. I. Sha'afi, S. B. Rodan, R. L. Hintz, <u>Nature</u> 254, 525
(1975).

9

Prenatal Diagnosis of the Hemoglobinopathies

David G. Nathan, Blanche P. Alter, and Maurice J. Mahoney

The prenatal diagnosis of the hemoglobinopathies became a realistic goal when Huehns and his associates (1) found evidence that hemoglobin A is present in small amounts in the red cells of the human fetus. Confirmation of this finding followed the application of sensitive techniques for measurement of hemoglobin A synthesis that employed radioisotopic labelling of the relevant hemoglobins or globin chains of the intact red cells of mid-trimester fetuses (2,3). In one study, heterozygosity for the sickle gene was detected in the cells of an aborted human fetus (3). These initial studies were rapidly expanded. The normal range of β chain synthesis relative to γ chain synthesis (the β/γ ratio) was defined in mid-trimester in order to make possible the detection of homozygous β thalassemia in fetal life (4,5). It was assumed that homozygous β thalassemia in the fetal red cell would be associated with extremely low production of β chain in such cells. That the latter assumption appeared to be true was determined by Chang and his co-workers (6) who studied mid-trimester aborted fetuses at risk either for β thalassemia trait or homozygous β thalassemia. In one of these fetuses the β/γ ratio was nearly zero suggesting that the low β/γ ratio observed in normal fetuses approaches zero in the fetus affected by homozygous β thalassemia.

Then began a series of clinical applications of this new technology. Two techniques to acquire fetal red cells were utilized (7,8). One, so-called placentocentesis, involved the localization of the placenta by ultrasound and the insertion of a #20 needle as close as possible to the fetal vessels that ramify on the chorionic plate. This is accomplished mainly by "feel." In the hands of skilled,or perhaps fortunate, operators, a high yield of fetal cells can be obtained, but the percentage of fetal cells is frequently very low. Furthermore, the number of attempts necessary to achieve an adequate sample often requires multiple

aspirations, increasing the danger of hemorrhage and
abruptio placenta. It is, however, a technique that requir
no special instrumentation other than ultrasonic placental
localization. An approach favored by our obstetrical
colleagues utilizes a 1.7 mm needlescope passed through a
2.2 mm trocar. The instrument contains a hard lens and
light source and a #27 needle. In all but the most strictl
anterior placentas, the chorionic surface can be approached
visually, a vein observed and the needle advanced directly
into the vein for the acquisition of a sample of nearly pur
fetal blood. Complications of this procedure have been
observed. They include persistent amniotic fluid leakage,
and there have been some reports of premature delivery and
fetal death. But in the hands of Hobbins and his co-worker
(8), the yield of fetal cells has been high and the fetal
morbidity and mortality low.

In the event of the production of a low yield sample,
the problem of maternal contamination of the fetal cells
can be a difficult one. In the case of either β thalassemi
or sickle cell disease, one searches for the absence of β^A
synthesis. Appreciable contamination of the sample with
maternal reticulocytes that synthesize β^A might well
obfuscate the findings. A sample from a homozygous deficie
fetus might appear to be consistent with either sickle or β
thalassemia trait. To deal with this problem, two approach
to the physical separation of the red cells from the sample
and one approach to the reduction of maternal reticulocytes
have been utilized. Maternal reticulocytes can be eliminat
from the placental circulation by hypertransfusion of the
mother one week prior to the procedure. This technique car
permit the use of very low yield samples because only the
maternal reticulocytes incorporate radioactivity into the
newly formed globin chains (9). However, this procedure
carries the risk of hepatitis and CMV infections. It is nc
a useful long term approach. One physical method of
separating maternal cells from fetal cells involves the use
of anti-i serum (10). A high titer antibody to the i antig
can certainly be used to agglutinate fetal cells and to cor
centrate them when they are present at a concentration of 1
or greater in the cell suspension. But there is often cros
agglutination with maternal cells and the yield may be low.
The technique has, however, been successfully used (11)
though it depends upon the availability of the reagent and
some skill in its use. More satisfactory is the recently
developed Ørskov technique for fetal cell concentration (12
This is more generally applicable. It depends upon the
relative deficiency of carbonic anhydrase in fetal cells
which, when acetazolamide is added to them, are rendered
nearly completely carbonic anhydrase deficient. Red cells

deficient in carbonic anhydrase do not lyse in the presence of ammonium chloride. Hence, exposure of a mixture of acetazolamide treated maternal and fetal cells to ammonium chloride results in the lysis of maternal cells and the recovery of intact fetal cells. Alter and her co-workers have shown that the Ørskov hemolysis technique permits a very accurate analysis of fetal globin synthesis in samples which initially contain as little as 2% fetal cells (13).

The application of these new technologies has been well received in centers in which large numbers of **couples** at risk **of** the birth of β thalassemic children abound.

Table 1 reviews the number of prenatal diagnoses that have been carried out for the hemoglobinopathies around the world as of **Feb.**, 1978. The Table indicates the site of obstetrical acquisition of cells,not necessarily the site of their biochemical manipulation.

Table 2 shows the results of studies in the Boston, New Haven and London axis in which the obstetrics have been carried out by fetoscopy in New Haven and placental aspiration in London. Biochemical determinations were performed in Boston. The fetal complications have been higher in the placental aspiration group and the yields of fetal red cells lower. There has been one false negative diagnosis in sickle cell disease in which a β peak was thought to be present that was actually merely a degradation product in a chromatogram (9). In a recent study of 24 cases (14), a clear distinction between homozygous β thalassemia and β thalassemia trait appeared to be possible in almost all cases and this is generally true. However, each diagnostic center does appear to have cases in which the fetal red cell β/γ ratio in homozygotes is not zero. It does, in fact, come quite close to the lower limits of the two standard deviations of the mean β/γ ratio in β thalassemia trait. Thus, the difference between β^0 thalassemia trait and homozygous β^+ thalassemia in the fetus may on occasion be difficult to determine. Most centers would err on the side of conservatism in that differential diagnosis.

Though the techniques described above are complex, they can be applied by well trained personnel. Couples at risk can look forward to having children of their own without fear; and in certain areas of the world where the population is well contained, it may, in fact, be possible to reduce the incidence of homozygosity. This would, of course, markedly reduce the impact of β thalassemia on the medical care economy in some parts of the world. However, the risks of injury to pregnancy remain relatively high, and an

Table 1

PRENATAL DIAGNOSIS OF HEMOGLOBINOPATHIES
JULY, 1974 – FEBRUARY, 1978

LONDON	103
NEW HAVEN	47
SAN FRANCISCO	43
SARDINIA	32
ATHENS	25
MUNICH	16
MELBOURNE	14
SAN ANTONIO	5
ISRAEL	3
BOSTON	2
TORONTO	1
MONTREAL	1
	292

Table 2

PRENATAL DIAGNOSIS OF HEMOGLOBINOPATHIES,
JULY, 1974-JUNE, 1978

	FETOSCOPY	ASPIRATION	TOTAL
TOTAL CASES	29	29	58
Fetal loss	2	5	7
Analyzable samples	27	24	51
Percent fetal cells	72	43	58
SICKLE DISORDERS	6	2	8
Analyzable samples	6	0	6
Homozygosity - established	3	0	3
- missed, born	1	0	1
Born - sickle trait	2	0	2
Still pregnant	0	0	0
THALASSEMIA	23	27	50
Analyzable samples	21	24	45
Homozygosity - established	1	4	5
Born - beta thalassemia trait	7	7	14
- alpha thalassemia trait	0	2	2
- normal	4	7	11
- diagnosis unknown	2	1	3
Still pregnant	4	0	4

improved, safer technology would be very desirable.

One such safer approach involves the use of fetal fibroblasts rather than reticulocytes for the detection of abnormalities of fetal globin gene expression that are due to gene deletion. Fetal fibroblasts are, in fact, a very adequate source for the detection of gene deletion syndromes The use of fluid phase DNA:cDNA molecular hybridization has been utilized to determine the number of α globin genes in the fetal fibroblast DNA (15). Very careful techniques have enabled Kan and his co-workers to distinguish between fetal hydrops fetalis, due to complete α chain deletion, and hemoglobin H disease in which 3 out of 4 genes are deleted. More recently, Orkin and his colleagues (16) have treated fibroblast DNA with certain restriction endonucleases followed by electrophoresis of digested fragments and quantitation of the globin genes in the fragments by in situ hybridization with globin cDNA. This method of gene quantitation has several advantages among which are a lower requirement for cellular DNA, visual inspection of results, and the use of α and β cDNA mixtures rather than purified α or β cDNA probes.

Currently, only gene deletion syndromes are capable of detection by the study of fetal fibroblasts. In the future it may be possible to detect the putative single base substitutions in DNA that cause low transcription of globin mRNA in β^+ and β^0 thalassemia. Another approach might involve the induction of globin gene transcription in fetal fibroblasts and the detection of errors of expression in that fashion. To date, fibroblasts have defied efforts to induce them to express their globin genes in a manner that would permit reliable prenatal diagnosis, but as progress in molecular and cell biology continues, couples at risk will be beneficiaries. It seems likely that recent advances will continue and a reliable and safe method will be forthcoming.

Editor's Note:

Subsequent to the preparation of this paper, Kan and Dozy (17) reported a new approach to the prenatal diagnosis of sickle cell anaemia or trait. Using the restriction endonuclease mapping technique, DNA from uncultured amniotic fluid cells was successfully split and analyzed and the fetus in question was found to have sickle cell trait. This confirmed the diagnosis made on the fetal blood sample.

References

1. Huehns, E.R., Dance, N., Beaven, G.H., Hecht, F. and Motulsky, A.G. Human embryonic hemoglobins. Cold Spring Harbor Symposia on Quantitative Biology, 29: 327-331, 1964.

2. Hollenberg, M.D., Kaback, M.M. and Kazazian, H.H. Adult hemoglobin synthesis by reticulocytes from the human fetus at midtrimester. Science 174:698-702, 1971.

3. Kan, Y.W., Dozy, A.M., Alter, B.P., Frigoletto, F.D. and Nathan, D.G. Detection of the sickle gene in the human fetus: Potential for intrauterine diagnosis of sickle cell anemia. New Engl J Med 287, 1-5, 1972.

4. Kazazian, H.H., Jr. and Woodhead, A.O. Adult hemoglobin synthesis in the human fetus. Annals of the New York Academy of Sciences 241, 691-698, 1974.

5. Cividalli, G., Nathan, D.G., Kan, Y.W., Santamarina, B., and Frigoletto, F. Relation of β to γ synthesis during the first trimester: An approach to prenatal diagnosis of thalassemia. Pediatric Research 8, 553-560, 1974.

6. Chang, H., Modell, C.B., Alter, B.P., Dickinson, M.J., Frigoletto, F.D., Huehns, E.R. and Nathan, D.G. Expression of the β-thalassemia gene in the first trimester fetus. Proceedings of the National Academy of Sciences of the United States of America 72:3633-3637, 1975.

7. Valenti, C. Antenatal detection of hemoglobinopathies A preliminary report. American Journal of Obstetrics and Gynecology, 115:851-853, 1973.

8. Hobbins, J.C., and Mahoney, M.J. In utero diagnosis of hemoglobinopathies. Technique for obtaining fetal blood.New England Journal of Medicine 290:1065-1067, 1974.

9. Alter, B.P., Modell, C.B., Fairweather, D., Hobbins, J.C., Mahoney, M.J., Frigoletto, F.D., Sherman, A.S. and Nathan, D.G. Prenatal diagnosis of hemoglobinopathies. A review of 15 cases. New England Journal of Medicine 295, 1437-1443, 1976

10. Kan, Y.W., Nathan, D.G., Cividalli, G. and Crookston, M.C. Concentration of fetal red blood cells from a mixture of maternal and fetal blood by anti-i serum--An aid to prenatal diagnosis of hemoglobinopathies. Blood, 43:411-415, 1974.

11. Kan, Y.W., Golbus, M.S., Klein, P. and Dozy, A.M. Successful application of prenatal diagnosis in a pregnancy at risk for homozygous β thalassemia. New England Journal of Medicine 292:1096-1099, 1975.

12. Boyer, S.H., Noyes, A.N. and Boyer, M.L. Enrichment of erythrocytes of fetal origin from adult-fetal blood mixtures via selective hemolysis of adult blood cells: an aid to antenatal diagnosis of hemoglobinopathies. Blood 47:883-897, 1976.

13. Alter, B.P., Metzger, J.B., Yock, P.G., Rothchild, S.B. and Dover, G.J. Selective hemolysis of adult red blood cells. An aid to prenatal diagnosis of hemoglobino- pathies. Manuscript submitted.

14. Kan, Y.W., Trecartin, R.F., Golbus, M.S. and Filly, R.A. Prenatal diagnosis of β thalassemia and sickle cell anemia. Experience with 24 cases. Lancet, 1, 269-271, 1977.

15. Kan, Y.W., Golbus, M.S. and Dozy, A.M. Prenatal diagnosis of α thalassemia. New England Journal of Medicine, 295:1165-1167, 1976.

16. Orkin, S.H., Alter, B.P., Altay, C., Mahoney, M.J., Lazarus, H., Hobbins, J.C. and Nathan, D.G. Application of endonuclease mapping to the analysis and prenatal diagnosis of thalassemias caused by globin gene deletion. New England Journal of Medicine, 299:166-172, 1978.

17. Kan, Y.W. and Dozy, A.M. Antenatal diagnosis of sickle cell anaemia by D.N.A. analysis os amniotic fluid cells. The Lancet, 910-912, Oct. 28, 1978.

Part III

Bridging the Gap Between Research and Practice

Educational Implications

10

A Place for Genetics
in Health Education
and Vice-Versa

Barton Childs

It is always the hope of geneticists to put discoveries
of the laboratory to use in the affairs of human beings.
Some expressions of these hopes have appeared in the recent
literature in the form of genetic engineering, reproductive
manipulation, germinal selection, and the like. These papers
reflect the view that while most of these methods will not
have wide application in the near future, their implied
threat to present mores requires some public debate to determine what is, or might become, acceptable, before eager investigators give them a life and impetus of their own.
These ideas have been advanced mainly by laboratory workers
who, moved by a strong social orientation, are prepared to
consider the biological manipulation of individuals as a
means of improvement of the whole society. Physicians, in
contrast, have greeted the new eugenics with suspicion or
indifference, no doubt for many reasons, but salient among
them is the fact that clinicians are seldom attentive to any-
thing beyond an individual patient's immediate problems, and
although the patient's family may be acknowledged as being in
their purview, the whole society is not.

These dissimilar views on the social benefits of genetic
knowledge may soon be moving toward reconcilliation, mainly,
I think, as a result of changes in medical thinking which
emphasize the prevention of disease and the preservation of
human biological and social equilibrium by means of an approach which is being called "health maintenance." There is
evidence, some of which I shall show, that genetics is not
being included in the formation of the content and the means
for furnishing this special kind of medical care, and it is
in the remedy of this deficiency that a common ground can be

Barton Childs, American Journal of Human Genetics, 26:120-135
1974. Copyright 1974 by the American Society of Human
Genetics and reproduced by permission. Univ. Chic. Press

found embracing both broad social aims and attention to the individual patient.

What is the means whereby this deficiency may be made up? I believe it not to be the new eugenics, which, in the remoteness of its application, is in any case of low immediate priority. In addition, while proposing the uses of genetics to improve genotypes, whether for individuals or for the whole species, it neglects to say how genetics can be used to improve the lot of genotypes already in existence. Nor will it be through further refinement of environmental manipulation (euphenics) to ameliorate the effects of harmful genes in persons already ill. Rather, it will come as a result of the discovery of the means to apply genetic knowledge universally and unselectively in the prevention of disease and the promotion of physical and emotional health.

In the fulfillment of this effort, we must find ways to minimize the adverse effects of some genes, some of which have been in the gene pool for a long time and will continue to be represented there, and to maximize the virtues of others which contribute adaptively, all in a rapidly changing environment.

Let me express the point another way. The net effect of civilization is greatly to increase the number of environments for which some genotypes will be unsuitable. Thus it might be said that the industrial revolution, while freeing human beings to enjoy the benefits of a technological society, has engendered a host of new genetical defects. Further, the increase in industrial, occupational, and cultural complexity is accompanied by a proliferation of physical and behavioral demands which should ultimately reveal the full range of innate variability. I suppose we have not yet achieved that ultimate, but we have come a long way. For example, the 1970 U.S. Census lists upwards of 23,000 occupations (1). This is about $2\frac{1}{2}$ times those listed in 1910, and although it is an impressive number, it still falls short of actuality, since many job headings include minor variations calling for differences in skills or allowing for greater or lesser exposure to health hazards. An editorial in a recent issue of the <u>Journal of Occupational Medicine</u>, commenting on a newly described occupational disease, revealed that there are already nearly 3,000 such disorders--a number, incidentally, which compares favorably with the number of genetic variations listed in McKusick's catalogue (2, 3). It would be interesting to know how many undiscovered overlaps already exist in the two lists, and even more so to know how many of the occupational disorders will be added, in their turn, to the genetical list.

If this concept were to be accepted by the medical profession, then an important dimension of health maintenance should consist of a genotypic description of each individual which should lead to some definition of his own adaptive and nonadaptive environments. This is not a particularly new idea, except insofar as it suggests rather precise refinements in the biological characterization of the attributes of roundness or squareness of pegs to be fitted into appropriate holes.

It might be questioned whether such a concept could be accepted by workers in the field of health, and 5 or more years ago it could not be, and was not, but the climate for it is much more favorable today, since medicine is undergoing a profound transformation in which acute and episodic medical care is giving way to prevention of disease and preservation and enhancement of health.

Modern Views of Medicine and Health

Sanitation, improved nutrition, rising living standards and medical care have reduced the incidence of acute illness and have lengthened life, but these boons have brought in their train an increasing incidence of the chronic illnesses of adult life which are presumed to represent the results of particular circumstances, habits, and modes of living, the kinds of disorders whose "risk factors" can be enumerated as age, sex, race, weight, and habits--dietary, smoking, and the like (4, 5). Treatments are--and probably will always be-- palliative, expensive, and profligate in use of medical care facilities and personnel, so that the obvious and most effective means of control should be preventive. This approach so far is more conceptual than overt, since the multifactorial origins of these diseases are not understood, but it is inescapable that they are strongly genetically influenced and represent the constitutional susceptibilities or diatheses which Archibald Garrod wrote about in his book Inborn Factors in Disease and which he suggested were no less the result of biochemical individuality than the inborn errors. (6).

The emergence of the chronic diseases represents a change in the quality of medical problems to be faced, but might not of itself have forced the changes in medicine which we are witnessing today. Of all the causes of these changes, perhaps the most potent is the idea that health is a right, open equally to all (7). This has produced a rising public expectation that scientific advances should be used, not only to treat disease, but to prevent it and to provide those social goods which, in addition to medical care, are necessary to promote and to achieve good health. So medicine is acquiring a pervasive social character in which the traditional physician in his one-to-one relationship with each patient is being augmented by instruments which preside over health, consisting of agencies and people with diverse skills who "deliver" a variety of elements of "medical care" and of "health maintenance." This means a greatly enhanced role for the practitioners of a wide range of special disciplines including: public health, occupational health, social health, health education, health behavior, and sociology and social work, as well as others whose activities are subsumed under such headings as medical care design, hospital administration, and the like, and whose business is the logistics of medicine.

It was pointed out in the Millis report that the need for physicians with these diverse skills strains the educational capacities of medical schools accustomed to graduating physicians all trained to do the same things; the system produces uniformity in the face of a need for variety (7). Medical schools have moved to fill this deficiency in both educational and research functions by the creation of new departments variously titled: community health, community medicine, social medicine, family practice, family medicine, preventive medicine, and medical care (8-10). In fact, of 104 medical schools in full operation and listed in the 1973 Association of American Medical Colleges directory, 78, or about three-fourths have departments listed under one or other of these names (11).

Among the concerns of these new departments is research into new ways to organize and provide medical care. One, among other outcomes of these investigations, is the Health Maintenance Organization (HMO) (12), which is a new name for prepaid group practice plans. "It is a system designed to bring health manpower, facilities, and consumers together into more effective relationships for meeting health care needs efficiently and in a manner convenient to provider and consumer. It places emphasis upon preventive services" (13). The theme here is an efficient working relationship between the purveyor and the recipient of services intended to promote health. The emphasis on the recipient in something other than a passive role is both new and important.

Thus, there are major conceptual changes taking place in which programs for health are to be made available for all without identifying particular individuals and in which the practitioner is no longer simply to wait in his office for the sick patient to present himself. These trends make it likely that future physicians will be more concerned with the

impact of civilization on the health of their patients, the
hazards of commercial products, and the adverse effects of
industry on the environment. In short, the time seems to be
coming when doctors, traditionally the most conservative and
parochial of people, may become advocates for health (14,15).

Genetics and the New Medicine

The geneticist will immediately see breathtaking oppor-
tunities in the new medicine. The ideas of prevention of
disease and promotion of good health are implicit in the
predictive function of genetics and have been explicitly
stated, at least since the 1930s (16). Indeed, the point was
clearly made by T. H. Morgan in his Nobel Prize address in
1935 (17). In those early days, the predictions had to stand
alone for lack of empirical data to attest to their accuracy.
Now, however, we have some clues in the rapidly growing sum
of evidences of the extent of human genetical variability in
health and disease (18). Harris has given us some idea of
the extent of polymorphism, and the association with diseases
of alleles of the HL-A and α_1-antitrypsin systems suggests
that mutants of the hemoglobin and G6PD loci may not be the
only polymorphic genes associated with disease (19, 20). Indeed, since the polymorphic alleles are the sources of the
common human differences, they must contribute strongly to
the susceptibilities which underlie the common chronic disorders now receiving so much medical attention.

As for more direct and obvious genic and chromosomal
causes of human disease, the literature abounds in testimony
to the proliferation of that knowledge, testimony derived
largely from representatives of this society and familiar to
all its members. The application of this knowledge to the
traditional care of sick patients need not concern us here.
The question I would like to examine is, To what extent does
genetics permeate the thinking and behavior of the participants of the transactions of health maintenance? If genetics
is to play much of a part, it will be because its pertinence
is recognized by professionals and public alike.

Medical Practice

No one would argue that genetics has not become integ-
rated into medical education and standard medical practice.
No less than 19 American medical schools have departments
of genetics or committees which fulfill that function (11).
Twenty-eight more have officially designated divisions of
genetics and 80% list required or elective courses in their
catalogues. Respectable treatment is accorded genetics in
text books, at least of medicine and pediatrics, and genetics

TABLE 1

Medical and Pediatric Journals Offer Ample Space for Papers on Genetics

Journal	No. Papers Published 1968-1972		
	Total	Genetic	% Genetic
J Clin Invest	1,422	179	12.59
Am J Med	959	119	12.41
Pediatrics	1,145	189	16.51
J Pediatr	1,499	372	25.67
Total	5,025	859	17.09

clinics are to be found in most, if not all, teaching hospitals. In addition, the research and clinical journals
give ample space to papers on genetical subjects (table 1).

While this is gratifying evidence that genetics is not
neglected, scrutiny of the titles and content of these papers
produces the realization that only a minority of them deal
with the distribution and frequencies of the genes in populations or with the characteristics of the gene pool of which
the qualities of populations are a reflection. That is, a
majority of the articles in the clinical literature deal with
genes and abnormal chromosomes as a cause of disease in specific persons and with their treatment and care. These publications are in the traditional medical vein of description
and management of disease and generally ignore population
genetics. And yet the appositeness of population genetics
to the new social-community-preventive medicine is obvious.

Obvious, but ignored.   I have found only the most
glancing references to genetics in the literature of these
new disciplines (8, 9). For example, Scientific American
devoted a whole number to "Life and Death in Medicine" with
little mention of genetics, while a symposium on community
medicine and heart disease, listing 12 papers which appeared
in the Bulletin of the New York Academy of Medicine, essentially ignored genetics, despite the obvious relationship of
the hereditary disorders of lipids with some cases of myo-
cardial infarction and the hereditary factors in the genesis
of hypertension (22, 23). A series of 19 articles on Health
Maintenance Organizations published in the Journal of Medical
Education was altogether innocent of any recognition of the
connection of population genetics and preventive medicine
(24).

Turning now to the literature of other medical and
health-related fields, one finds almost no attention to
genetics. This is substantiated by looking at the titles of
the papers which filled a number of journals the period
1968-1972. If the title was ambiguous or unrevealing, the
paper was scanned until I was satisfied it did or did not
contain some genetical content. I am aware that journals
cannot reflect precisely the most current ideas, but they
must contain the prevailing opinions and views of their con-
stituents (table 2).

In the public health journals there were a number of
papers on the adverse effects of radiation, but little
about screening, antenatal diagnosis, or counseling. The
journals of environmental and occupational medicine contained even fewer genetical works, despite many reports of

TABLE 2

Journals in Several Medical and Allied Fields Publish Only Occasional Articles
with Genetic Content, or None at All

| | No. Papers Published 1968-1972 | | |
Journal	Total	Genetic	% Genetic
Am J Public Health	981	12	1.22
Health Serv Rep	649	8	1.23
Br J Prev Soc Med	198	6	3.03
Am J Epidemiol	616	11	1.79
Med Care	235	0	0.00
Arch Environ Health	957	23	2.40
J Occup Med	452	4	0.88
Ann Occup Hyg	173	1	0.58
Br J Ind Med	255	2	0.78
Ind Med Surg	342	3	0.87
Am Ind Hyg Assoc J	499	1	0.20
Soc Sci Med	275	1	0.36
J Health Soc Behav	175	0	0.00
Soc Casework	273	1	0.37
Br J Sociol	158	0	0.00
Am J Sociol	225	1	0.44
Am Sociol Rev	231	0	0.00
J Sch Health	481	6	1.25

exposure to almost numberless agents of just the sort the geneticist might expect to be hazardous to some and not to others. The sociological journals, whether or not, contained almost no genetical papers, despite the social problems raised by screening, antenatal diagnosis, and counseling. Finally, although the Journal of School Health seemed preoccupied mainly with drugs and smoking and with programs of education for health, there were two enlightening papers outlining the value of some knowledge of genetics in preventive medicine and in promoting good health. So it is apparent that little attention to genetics is paid by proponents of community-family-preventive medicine or by investigators in public health, occupational and industrial medicine, school health, and medical sociology, and yet these fields must be the portals through which population genetics would most naturally be introduced and the natural ways in which the social aims of genetics would be realized.

What this seems to mean is that people concerned with the effects of the environment on health, with the prevention of overt disease and the maintenance and enhancement of health, do their work with only occasional reference to possible genetical origins of the difference between the people they serve, or to the chance that these genetical differences might be critical for the appropriate disposition of specific individuals. Preventive measures are of little use to non-susceptible persons, while to discover those who are liable to the injury to be prevented is to make sure that they are not exposed at all. To omit to take innate propensities into account in preventive medicine is to make rules which in presuming to suit all may suit none, or which at the least impose unnecessary constraints upon nonsusceptible persons.

Education in Genetics for Physicians and the Public

The lack of reference to genetics in the journals reviewed is surely a reflection of a deficiency of convincing empirical evidence and a lack of practical experience with genetical characteristics and diseases. But these journals carry reports of the research done in these fields and the lack of articles of a theoretical or pioneering nature suggests that physicians in preventive medicine, public health, and environmental medicine do not think genetically. If so, we may ask whether population genetics, as it is currently being taught in medical school, will fill this gap. Further, if one believes that genetics is essential for the successful outcome of the new medicine, then one must ask whether its beneficiaries, the patients, will have the foundation of knowledge required to allow them that participation so often proclaimed as one of its pillars.

Medical Teaching

Population genetics is always accorded a place in the course on human genetics given in medical schools and it is usually given, as indeed it must be, a strongly mathematical treatment. On the other hand, insufficient attention is often paid to its meaning to patients and medical practice. This is partly due to a lack of those empirical data which illuminate a mathematical argument for the nonmathematician, and partly because genetics in medical schools is grouped among the preclinical sciences. The course is usually given in the first year, and those schools whose emphasis on genetics is attested by required courses, departments, and divisions turn out to be the same ones whose faculties engage in and stress research, while those whose emphasis is on patient care and whose avowed purpose is to produce practitioners tend to accord genetics a lukewarm reception or to ignore it (25). Further, there is a strong negative correlation in medical schools between the possession of departments and divisions of genetics and departments of community and preventive medicine (25). All this means that population genetics is given little or no attention in some schools, and in those places where its value is acknowledged, its concepts are given little reinforcement in the clinical years.

The Public

I know of no comprehensive study of the extent of the public's knowledge, or even awareness, of genetics; it would be a study of much interest and use. A few papers have appeared, however, mainly during the past 2 years, which suggest that many people are ignorant of genetics and that there are problems of grasp, even when the lesson appropriate for their particular disorder is given them (26-33). The results presented in these papers, embracing phenylketonuria, cystic fibrosis, mongolism, congenital heart disease, hemophilia, sickle cell disease, Werdnig-Hoffman's disease, and others, may be telling us that a significant part of the difficulty these parents had in receiving and remembering what they were told consists of an inadequate foundation on which to impose a coherent account of the disease and its pattern of inheritance. Favoring this view is the significant relationship between intelligence and previous educational attainment and the ability to grasp and to remember genetic knowledge, including probabilities (33, 34). On the other hand, the papers also suggest that the facts may not be received at all, may be misinterpreted, or may be ignored, depending upon a person's perception of the relationship of those facts to himself and to his life. Thus, there appear to be two levels of knowledge which a human being requires to deal rationally with genetics. Both are necessary, but neither alone is sufficient for rational judgment and decision. This is borne out in the large literature on patients' compliance with doctors' directions (35, 36). These studies, mainly testing conformity with instructions to take drugs by patients with all degrees of illness, showed that on the average about one-third of the patients paid little heed to the doctor's orders, and this figure rose in some reports to as much as 85%. Again, these studies give evidence that while nothing can be done unless the facts are clearly grasped, beyond this some insight and psychological engagement on the part of both doctor and patient are also required.

Education in genetics for the general public appears to be scanty. Several foundations, the American Medical Association, and other medical organizations furnish pamphlets, articles, films, and other material including television spots, often in conjunction with fund raising. Disease-related foundations also supply educational help to the victims or families of patients with genetic diseases.

The mass media, taking their educational responsibilities lightly, publish articles on genetic disease or counseling, some of which are good, while some, for example "The Obsolescent Mother" which appeared in the Atlantic, are only sensational (37). To see what the affluent middle-brow who reads Time magazine would learn, I looked at the articles which appeared under the headings "Medicine" and "Science" during the 4 years, 1969-1972 (38), table 3. Under "Medicine" there were 303 articles, of which 12 were genetical in content, while of 272 articles labeled "Science," there were six. With the possible exception of an article entitled "The New Genetics, Man into Superman," and one which engenders the illusion of an effective treatment of sickle cell anemia, none of the articles is of itself unworthy, but the rarity of the diseases and the recondite nature of the molecular biology which supply their content cause me to wonder in what context the reader is able to view them and to comprehend them.

Genetics in Primary and Secondary Schools

Subsequent generations will be much more knowledgeable in genetics than present ones, due to the transformation of the teaching of science in primary and secondary schools, said to be a consequence of the space rivalry with the Soviet Union. Even a superficial review of science teaching in schools reveals a very encouraging acceptance of science as the equal of more traditional subjects and the availability of thoughtful and well constructed courses which begin in the

TABLE 3

Subjects of Articles Which Appeared in _Time Magazine_ under the Headings
Medicine and Science, 1969-1972

Medicine	Science
Thymic Transplantation	Cattle Breeding
Mental Retardation	Transformation of Gal-Cells by Virus
Spinal Cerebellar Degeneration	Khorana's Synthetic Gene
"The New Genetics: Man into Superman"	Reverse Transcriptase
Tay-Sachs Screening	Electron Microscopy of DNA
Treatment of Sickle Cell Anemia	Isolation of Lac Operon
Dermatoglyphics	
Porphyria in the British Royal Family	
Transplantation Rejection	
Hexosaminidase A Deficiency	
Amniocentesis and Antenatal Diagnosis	
Nobel Prize Winners for 1969	

kindergarten and are sustained through twelfth grade. Genetics is given a place of prominence here and the universal application of its principles is given appropriate emphasis (39-44). Furthermore, scientific principles are seen to be within the grasp of all but a few school children.

There seems to me to be only one failing in this and that is one of omission. That is the anatomy, physiology, and development of man is given relatively little space, especially in the elementary school texts, and when it does appear it is often out of context and rather diffidently or awkwardly treated, or sometimes it is offered in the form of health-related homilies about washing hands, or having immunizations, the kinds of things the teacher may regard as hygiene (table 4).

It must be acknowledged that separate courses in human biology are given in some schools, and that many imaginative teachers augment and enliven the standard texts, but it must be a rare child in our schools who is given a coherent idea of his own origins, or of how his body works, what he may expect of it, and how he differs from other people.

Some attempt is made to fill the need by efforts to teach the meaning of good health and how to attain and keep it; but although the School Health Education Study group is making a strong and positive effort to update and otherwise improve this field by designing courses to be given from kindergarten through twelfth grade, and other educators agitate for time and teachers, school health education still too often remains in the reluctant hands of departments of physical education who give instruction in hygiene, nutrition, posture, and reproduction, as well as the evils of smoking, drugs, and venereal infections (45-47).

To summarize, while public education in biology and genetics is incomparably better than only a few years ago, the enlightened participation of the mass of people in preventive programs for health seems still to require that the teaching in school be more specifically oriented to providing that basis upon which specific details of knowledge of disease and health may be later imposed.

What Is To Be Done?

If these deficiencies really matter, they will be made up in time, motivated by the exigencies of preventive medical care, but such a result could only come piecemeal and without coherence. An alternative might be an attack on several fronts at once, with the aim of weaving genetics into the

TABLE 4

Science Texts for Elementary School Students Do Not Expose Children
to Much Human Biology

Title and Publisher	No. Volumes Examined	No. Pages Total	No. Pages Human Biology	% Human Biology
Concepts in Science, Harcourt Brace	6	1,723	78	4.5
Science, Silver, Burdett	6	1,315	120	9.1
World of Science, Bobbs-Merrill	6	1,488	93	6.3
Science for Tomorrow's World, MacMillan*	5	1,246	253	20.3
Science for You, Ginn	5	1,081	30	2.8
Basic Science Program, Scott-Foresman	6	1,183	43	3.6
Total	34	8,036	617	7.7

*Dr. Benjamin Spock was a member of the editorial board.

conceptual fabric of health maintenance for physicians and patients alike.

Teaching Population Genetics

The first question is where in medical schools to teach "practical" population genetics and in what context.

The obvious setting is those very departments of preventive medicine, community health, and family practice which, as we have seen, lack knowledge or even much awareness of genetics. The preoccupation with the effects of environmental influences on human health, their concern with prevention of disease and the preservation of health, their interest in developing affinities with the objects of medical care, namely people, families, and other community elements, their knowledge of the economics and logistics of medicine and their use of epidemiological methods in research all conspire to suit them for this responsibility.

A convincing medical context appears to be emerging in the discovery of the extent of human polymorphism, and the relationship of polymorphic alleles to disease, as well as in the growth of programs for screening for genetical disorders with the intention to institute treatment or to give advice about preventive options. As these practices increase, the connection between the distributions and frequencies of genes and diseases will become the focus of much more medical interest.

The next question is how to put the cause of population genetics before its potential teachers, as well as other physicians engaged in public health, occupational and industrial medicine, and the like. We may be sure that it cannot be done by talks such as this one, by preaching to the converted, or by publications which appear in the genetics literature. We shall have to find ways to carry the message to those places where it will have the most effect. The sociologists tell us that an innovation is most rapidly disseminated if it can be brought to the attention of, and is taken up by, the opinion leaders of the field in question (48-50). Opinion leaders are those weighty members of the Establishment whose views are heeded by lesser folk. They are generally conservative, opinionated, and slow to change, but they represent and mold prevailing opinion, and if they accept a new idea, it is likely soon to become the standard view. Who are the relevant opinion leaders and how can they be infleunced? They are the professors and chairmen of departments of community health, family medicine, and so on; directors of the large prepaid medical groups, such as

Kaiser-Permanente; deans of medical schools and schools of
public health; state and city public health officials; and
the money men at the National Institutes of Health and private foundations, including the disease-oriented foundations
How can they be approached? Directly, by members of this
society in their roles as faculty or as members of national
societies and advisory bodies, whether to the National Institutes of Health or other organizations; by appropriately
placed reviews, articles, or editorials, especially in journals read by those to be influenced; by offering fellowships
in genetics to people with degrees in epidemiology or public
health; and possibly in the meetings of this society. For
example, the American Society of Human Genetics might sponsor
a meeting on some aspects of the applications of population
genetics to, say, preventive medicine, possibly in conjunction with its annual gathering, with participants to be in-
vited from among the "opinion leaders" to be influenced, as
well as from the society. The proponents of preventive medicine and health maintenance would give us their thoughts and
we would give them ours. Whatever ways are tried, they will
be successful in the degree to which members of the human
genetics establishment see the continuing education of our
colleagues as part of our work.

    As a second priority among medical educators to influ-
ence, I suggest the movers and shakers of the new schools of
allied health sciences. These schools will have strong effects on the personnel who will man the Health Maintenance
Organizations and comprehensive care clinics, people who will
occupy a primary position as educators and counselors to the
public in preventive medicine and health behavior. I have no
data on the place of genetics in the minds and programs of
the developers and functionaries of these schools; it bears
looking into, but experience suggests it will be neglected.

The Public

    As for the adult public, the job is a difficult one and
expectations should be trimmed to fit possibilities. Education designed to change lifelong habits is notoriously difficult and depressingly often unsuccessful. Because of this,
and in response to the increasing complexity of the medical
scene, new kinds of efforts are being made to help people
learn the significance to them of medical care.

    Health education is relatively new. One it consisted
merely of handing out pamphlets in outpatient departments and
in exhibiting posters and charts. Then someone noticed that
these measures fell short of desirable achievement and began
to investigate what might be required to persuade people

voluntarily to do things which maintain and enhance their own health. To this end it has been necessary to use the methods of the behavioral and social sciences, and investigators of health education and behavior tend to have those viewpoints.

One result is the recognition of differences in behavior of patients in sickness and in health (51-53). A patient who perceives himself to be sick may be willing to surrender himself to the care of his doctor, but a healthy person requires to be convinced of the usefulness of preventive measures and usually must himself take active steps to obtain them. He is likely to do so if he perceives the seriousness of the condition to be prevented, and recognizes his own susceptibility. He will not do so if these perceptions are beclouded by lack of knowledge or other barriers to action. Further, it is a well-known human failing to neglect to act, even on rational grounds, without some sharply focused, sometimes painful, impulse.

All this sounds so self-evident. In the instance of genetical diseases, one has only to tell the potential screenee or counselee that the condition they face is a bad one, that they have a specific susceptibility, and that particular steps will lead to prevention, or that they now have the wherewithal to make a sensible reproductive decision. But we all know it is not so simple, and I suggest that it is in the discovery of the many reasons why it is not simple that the viewpoint and methods of health educators may be of help to the geneticist. As it happens, the papers of workers in health education and behavior reveal no recognition of genetical problems, but the record of research by geneticists into the successes and failures of counseling, screening, and antenatal diagnosis is also poor in references to the experts in health education. Some collaboration, on the other hand, could not fail to help in studies of the impact of educational efforts to apprise the public of the use and availability of preventive services, of the barriers which inhibit some people from accepting them, and of the cues which trigger the actions of those who do. Such investigations are essential, since the success of a preventive effort is measured directly by the proportion of the population at risk who avail themselves of it. Probably no preventive program should be undertaken without such validating studies as an integral part of the service.

As the results of this research accumulate, they may suggest the factual content and the context in which to present it which will lead to successful education for adults in genetics.

For children, we have seen that science teaching has entered a period of fruitful and diverse proliferation. It remains to capitalize on that impetus, and in doing so, some organized medical and genetics institutions ought to play a leading part.

I say medical institutions here, not for any parochial reason. Indeed, medical professionalism may be one of the factors which has inhibited the teaching of human biology in the past. But medical schools are the only schools of human biology, and short of sweeping structural changes in institutions of higher learning, they will continue to be, and as such must accept some responsibility for the design and organization of teaching in human biology. Since in the past clinicians have shown neither awareness of duty nor aptitude for this work, they are unlikely to do so now. Perhaps this is another job for the schools of allied health sciences, who might organize medical school resources, as well as their own, to design new courses in human biology for primary and secondary school students, and undertake to teach the teachers as well. Other possibilities are those universities which have brought together faculty from medicine and biology to form programs and give degrees in human biology. A possible career for a doctoral product of such programs might be in research in human biology education for school children. Others who might become engaged, especially in teaching genetics, perhaps in the schools of allied health sciences, are the graduates of the schools of genetic counseling, for example those at Sarah Lawrence or Rutgers.

There is precedent for involvement of university faculty in lower school teaching. The International Clearinghouse on Science and Mathematics Curricular Developments lists experiments in curriculum design for elementary and secondary schools from all over the world (54). There are 111 science projects listed in the United States, of which about two-thirds are entirely or mainly biological, and a further 33 in mathematics. These courses are the work of thoughtful and inventive educators, mainly members of university departments of biology, chemistry, physics, and mathematics, who were given financial support by the American Association for the Advancement of Science, the National Science Foundation, the U.S. Office of Education, and others. These scientists were motivated by their recognition of the inadequacy of science teaching, first in secondary school, then all the way down to the kindergarten. Why should medical faculty do any less?

Whatever is done, whether in conformity with these suggestions or with others, there must be some degree of reorientation in the approach to science teaching in schools. As

it is, except in those instances in which the teachers are
unusually perceptive and orignial, the teaching of science,
including biology--and possibly above all genetics with its
emphasis on probability--cultivates too little awareness of
its social significance. The teaching is disciplinary and
can be quickly learned and as quickly forgotten. The dis-
crepancy between the discipline-oriented teaching received
in school and the mission-oriented activities of contemporary
and later life creates that sense of dissonance in the minds
of some students which leads in cries for "relevance" or engenders apathy (55). It is this mission-oriented ingredient
which the medical school can and should inject into teaching
of human biology and genetics in schools. If the people are
truly to participate with physicians in the preservation and
enhancement of their health, rather than supinely to accept
the doctor's orders or irrationally to reject them, a sense
of this responsibility and the knowledge to execute it must
be cultivated from early childhood. This cannot be accomplished if school is perceived by children to be unconnected
with living,. or if courses in education about health are perceived to be unrelated to those in biology.

Conclusion

Francis Galton is known as the inventor of the idea that
selective breeding would bring worthwhile social benefits.
It is little known, however, that he was not in favor of beginning on such a course until its wisdom could be shown.
He said: "When the desired fullness of information shall
have been acquired, then, and not till then, will be the fit
moment to proclaim a holy war against customs and prejudices
that impair the physical and moral qualities of our race"
(56). Most of us would agree that we have not the "desired
fullness of information," and I doubt we ever will, but the
path of evolution medicine has taken offers genetics a favorable context in which to develop an approach to a different
galtonian end; to wit, the means to help people to make capital of genetical advantages and to skirt the genetical traps
which lurk in their own chromosomes. This requires no less
public collaboration than other preventive medical measures,
and no less knowledge, together with the understanding to use
it wisely. To this end, medical geneticists must help to educate both their medical colleagues and the public, hoping to
build in the latter some structural skeleton of information
in which the details of particular medical and genetical
circumstances could be applied in easy comprehension. One
wonders why we are so late in doing so, why the biology of
man has not been a primary object of education. The causes
of this omission would make an absorbing study which has apparently not been done, but whatever they are, the lack has

not gone unnoticed, having been remarked, for example, by
Thomas Huxley, who in many papers returned again and again to
the point. I will give only one example. It is taken from
an essay entitled "On Elementary Instruction in Physiology"
published in 1877, 96 years ago (57). It reads: "It is, I
think, eminently desirable that the hygienist and the physician should find something in the public mind to which they
can appeal; some little stock of universally acknowledged
truths, which may serve as a foundation for their warnings,
and predispose towards an intelligent obedience in their
recommendations."

References

1. Bureau of the Census, U. S. Dept. of Commerce. Classified Index of Industries and Occupations. Washington, D.C., U.S. Government Printing Office, 1971

2. McCord, C.P.: A new occupational disease is born. J. Occup. Dis. 12:234, 1970

3. McKusick, V.A.: Mendelian Inheritance in Man, 3d ed. Baltimore, Johns Hopkins Press, 1971

4. Glazier, W.H.: The task of medicine. Sci. Am. 228: 13, 1973

5. White, K.L.: Life and death and medicine. Sci. Am. 229: 23, 1973

6. Garrod, A.E.: Inborn Factors in Disease. Oxford, Oxford University Press, 1931

7. Millis, J.S.: A Rational Public Policy for Medical Education and Its Financing. New York, National Fund for Medical Education, 1971

8. Challenor, B.D., Wicks, J., Lythcott, G.I.: Community Medicine: an evolving discipline. Am. Intern Med. 76: 698, 1972

9. Ranson, D.C., Vandervoort, H.E.: The development of family medicine: problematic trends. JAMA 225:1098, 1973

10. Silver, G.A.: The teaching of social medicine. Clin. Res 21:151, 1973

11. AAMC Directory of American Medical Education, 1972-1973. Washington, D.C., Association of American Medical Colleges.

12. Wilson, V.E.: HMOs: hopes and aspirations. J. Med. Educ 48:7, 1973

13. Willard, W.R.: Ideals and realities of academic medical center involvement with HMOs. J. Med. Educ. 48:13, 1973

14. Nader, R.: Responsibility of physicians to society. Fed. Proc. 31:1578, 1972

15. Mechanic, D.: Sociology and public health: perspectives for application. Am. J. Public Health 64:146, 1972

16. Macklin, M.D.: Heredity and the physician. Sci. Monthly 52:56, 1941

17. Morgan, T.H.: The relation of genetics to physiology and medicine. Sci. Monthly 41:5, 1935

18. Harris, H., Hopkinson, D.A.: Average heterozygosity per locus in man; an estimate based on the incidence of enzyme polymorphism. Am. Hum. Genet. 36:9, 1972

19. Alper, C.A.: Deficiency of alpha-antirypsin. Am. Intern. Med. 78:298, 1973

20. Schlosstein, L., Terasaki, P.I., Bluestone, R., Pearson, C.M.: High association of HL-A antigen W27 with ankylosing spondylitis. N.Eng.J.Med. 288:704,1973

21. Deuschle, K.W.: The concept of community medicine and heart disease. Bull. N.Y. Acad. Med. 29:451, 1973

22. Sci. Am., vol. 229, no. 3, September 1973

23. Bull. N.Y. Acad. Sci., vol. 49, no. 6, 1973

24. J. Med. Educ., vol 48, no. 4, pt. 2, 1973

25. Childs, B.: Galton, and clinical medicine. Yale J. Biol. Med. In press, 1974

26. Sibinga, M.S., Freidman, C.J.: Complexities of parental understanding of phenylketonuria. Pediatrics 48:216, 1971

27. McCrae, W.M., Cull, A.M., Burton, L., Dodge, J.: Cystic fibrosis: paretns' response to the genetic basis of the disease. Lancet 2:141, 1973

28. Leonard, C.O., Chase, G., Childs, B.: Genetic counseling: a consumer's view. N. Eng. J. Med. 287:433, 1972

29. Reiss, J.A., Menashe, V.D.: Genetic counseling and congenital heart disease. J. Pediatr. 80:655, 1972

30. Taylor, K., Merrill, R.E.: Progress in the delivery of health care. Am. J. Dis. Child. 119:209, 1970

31. Hampton, M.L., Lavizzo, B.S., Anderson, J.R., Bergman, A.B.: Sickle cell non-disease--a potentially serious public health problem. Transactions of the Ambulatory Pediatric Association, 13th annual meeting, San Francisco, May 16-17, 1973

32. Pearn, J.H., Wilson, J.: Acute Werdnig-Hoffman disease. Arch. Dis. Child 48:425, 1973

33. Pearn, J.H.:Patients' subjective interpretation of risks offered in genetic counseling. J. Med. Genet. 10:129, 1973

34. Carter, C.O., Fraser Roberts, J.A., Evans, K.A., Buck, A.R.: Genetic clinic: a follow-up. Lancet 1:281, 1971

35. Blackwell, B.: Drug therapy: patient compliance. N. Eng. J. Med 289:249, 1973

36. Marston, M-V.: Compliance with medical regimes: a review of the literature. Nurs. Res. 19:312, 1970

37. Grossman, E.: The obsolescent mother. Atlantic 277:39, 1971

38. Time, vols. 93-100, 1969-1972

39. Brandwein, P.F., Cooper, E.K., Blackwood, P.E., Hone, E.B.: Concepts in Science, 2d ed. vols. 1-6, New York, Harcourt Brace, 1970

40. Mallinson, G.G., Mallinson, J.B., Ellwood, E.P., Zeiger, L., Feravola, R., Trexler, C.R., Brown, D.G.. Smallwood, W.L.: Science, vols. 1-6. Morristown, N.J., Silver, Burdett, 1968

41. Novak, J.D., Meister, M., Knox, W.W., Sullivan, D.W.: World of Science Series, vols. 1-6. Indianapolis, Bobbs-Merrill, 1966

42. Seltzer, S., ed.: Science for Tomorrow's World, vols. 1-5. New York, Macmillan, 1966

43. Craig, G.S., Bryan, B.E.: Science for You, vols. 1-5, Boston, Ginn, 1965

44. Marshall, J.S., Beauchamp, W.L.: The Basic Science Program, vols. 1-6. Chicago, Scott-Foresman, 1965

45. Southworth, W.H.: Health education from kindergarten through college. J. Sch. Health 38:193, 1968

46. Lussier, R.R.: Health education and student needs. J. Sch. Health 42:618, 1972

47. Sorochan, W.D.: Health instruction--why do we need it in the '70s? J. Sch. Health 41:209, 1971

48. Rogers, E.M., Shoemaker, F.: Communication of Innovations, 2d ed. New York, Free Press, 1971

49. Becker, M.H.: Predictors of innovative behavior among health officers. Public Health Rep. 84:1063, 1969

50. Becker, M.H.: Factors affecting diffusion of innovations among health professionals. Am. J. Public Health 60:294, 1970

51. Rosenstock, I.M.: Why people use health services. Milbank Mem. Fund Q.44:94, 1966

52. Kasl, S.V., Cobb, S.: Health behavior, illness behavior and sick role behavior. Arch. Environ. Health 12:246, 1966

53. Green, L.W.: Should health education abandon attitude change strategies? Perspectives for recent research. Health Educ. Monograph 30:25, 1970

54. Lockard, J.D., ed.: Eighth Report of the International Clearinghouse on Science and Mathematics Curricular Developments. Committee on Science Education, American Association for the Advancement of Science and Science Teaching Center, University of Maryland, 1973

55. Ashby, E.: The Bernal Lecture. Science and antiscience Proc. R. Soc. Land (Biol) 178:29, 1972

56. Pearson, K.: The Life, Letters, and Labours of Francis Galton, vol. 2. Cambridge, Cambridge University Press, 1914

57. Huxley, T.H.: Science and Education. New York, Philosophical Library, 1964